Mr. Right Now

Mr. Right Now

WHEN DATING IS BETTER THAN SAYING "I DO"

RACHEL SAFIER

JOSSEY-BASS
A Wiley Company
San Francisco

Published by Jossey-Bass
A Wiley Imprint
989 Market Street, San Francisco, CA 94103-1741   www.josseybass.com

Jossey-Bass books and products are available through most bookstores. To contact
Jossey-Bass directly call our Customer Care Department within the U.S. at
800-956-7739, outside the U.S. at 317-572-3986, or fax 317-572-4002.

Jossey-Bass also publishes its books in a variety of electronic formats. Some con-
tent that appears in print may not be available in electronic books.

Excerpt from *When Harry Met Sally* granted courtesy of Castle Rock
Entertainment.

Pages 169–70 from *The Art of Love* from *The Erotic Poems* by Ovid,
translated by Peter Green (Penguin Classics, 1982). Copyright © Peter Green,
1982. Reproduced by permission of Penguin Books Ltd.

The fact that an organization or Web site is referred to in this work as a citation
and/or a potential source of further information does not mean that the author or
the publisher endorses the information the organization or Web site may provide
or recommendations it may make. Further, readers should be aware that Internet
Web sites listed in this work may have changed or disappeared between when this
work was written and when it is read.

Library of Congress Cataloging-in-Publication Data
Safier, Rachel, date.
   Mr. Right Now : when dating is better than saying "I do" / Rachel
Safier.—1st ed.
      p. cm.
Includes bibliographical references.
   ISBN 0-7879-7127-8 (alk. paper)
   1. Single women—Psychology.   2. Man-woman relationships.   I. Title.
HQ800.2.S25 2004
306.7—dc22
                                      2003021203

Printed in the United States of America
FIRST EDITION
PB Printing   10 9 8 7 6 5 4 3 2 1

Contents

For my father

Acknowledgments

My heartfelt appreciation to Alan Rinzler and Catherine Craddock of Jossey-Bass; Stacey Glick of Dystel-Goderich Literary Management; David Blasband; contributing therapists Jennie Ackerman, Marci Drimer, Ruth Greer, Leigh Heerema, Eric Levin, Michael Lunter, Deborah Shelkrot Permut, Sonya Rencevicz, Lisa Slade-Martin, and Miriam Stern; my model friends Michael Blake, Brett Heimov, and Dan Singer; the women who shared their stories with me; and of course, the Misters.

Mr. Right Now

Introduction

So you've always thought you'd get married. And since you read the papers, watch the news and reality shows, and take calls from your mother, you're pretty worried about the fact that you haven't walked down the aisle yet. The self-help shelves at your local bookstore are crammed with alarmist titles like *Stop Getting Dumped* and *Gentlemen Prefer Blondes but Gentlemen Marry Brunettes*. Voices on all sides are telling you to hurry the hell up, and while you're at it, don't act too desperate. You've gotten to the point where you think you're not being proactive enough. You may be wondering if it's time to dig deep and buy *Find a Husband After 35 Using What I Learned at Harvard Business School: A Simple 15-Step Action Program* so you can follow the author's plan for finding a mate. (It's a plan that *Publisher's Weekly* called "time consuming, financially taxing and sometimes nearly humiliating,"[1] but don't let that deter you.) A little voice inside you is peeping, "Maybe you've missed your chance."

To put it mildly, you're edgy.

THE PRESSURE TO MARRY

Sure, you've got your college diploma, maybe a graduate degree or two, and even a satisfying career. But all you've achieved is nothing without a man, according to Wendy L. Walsh, who recounts her sad, manless existence in *The*

Boyfriend Test: How to Evaluate His Potential Before You Lose Your Heart:

> I was in acute pain, though on the outside you couldn't see that. I was a reporter and host on the national magazine show *Extra*. I was developing my own television production company. I was helping to run a charity. I was chairing a women's investment group, and I was buying and remodeling my first home. . . . [But t]his hectic schedule was just a mask, a way to keep busy, to hold back my tears.[2]

In the old days it seemed so easy. Mom married Dad long before her thirtieth birthday, and all her sisters married young too. Fast-forward a few decades and here you are, wondering, "If I'm so wonderful why am I still single?" And there's your question, right there on the bookstore shelf, now the title of a self-help book by Susan Page (the subtitle is *Ten Strategies That Will Change Your Life Forever*)—one of the plethora aimed at single-and-looking (read "desperate") women.

It seemed easier in the past, in part because matchmaking was once society's business, writes social historian Barbara Dafoe Whitehead in *Why There Are No Good Men Left*. Now individuals are expected to shoulder the burden. Where college was once as much about getting your MRS degree as an education, she says, it's now solely about preparing women for financial independence. But women are up to the task at hand. According to Whitehead, we're rolling up our sleeves and "taking a more focused, organized, professional approach to the search for love. . . ."[3]

Whitehead's grimace-and-bear-it approach to finding your ultimate mate may sound practical, but why does dating have to feel so much like crisis management? My answer: It doesn't have to.

MOVING FROM BREAKING UP TO HAVING A REALLY GOOD TIME

The success of my first book, *There Goes The Bride*, made me the breakup expert from New York to London. Now the men I meet have two questions for me: Do I believe in love? And do they run the risk of turning up in one of my books? (Yes and yes. But don't worry—everyone gets pseudonyms in my books.)

I do believe in love, though I can understand how the label of "breakup expert" could conjure up thoughts of a woman laughing devilishly every time she hears about another breakup, whether of good friends or some Hollywood power couple.

I do believe in love, and yet here I am, "alone" and happy. I'm thirty-three, "getting on" to some. I'm running the terrible risk of dying alone, as one conservative marriage expert actually told me. So how can I be so insouciant?

I've got a wager for you. I'm willing to bet that my chances of getting married in the next five years and of having a deep, enduring relationship with that still-unknown man are just as good as if not better than yours, if you're one of the millions of women standing in the self-help aisle freaking out. And I know without a shadow of a doubt that I'm enjoying myself more. You're taking notes in the margins of

The Best Advice on Finding Mr. Right and *The Rules,* and I'm living my life. You're glued to scary media reports to validate your feelings about being unmarried. You're looking to "experts" to stop the anxiety by telling you how to get married.

And I'm here to tell you to take a deep breath.

Step away from the self-help stack.

Turn off the TV.

Tell your mom you'll call her back.

The way to stop the anxiety is to refuse to give in to the hype.

There is no rush. You can afford to wait. You should wait. And every relationship you have had so far is the exact opposite of a waste of time. Every relationship you experience is enhancing your life, developing your senses, helping you realize what—just as much as who—you want in your life. Every relationship you sample is important, even those that don't end with the man on bended knee begging you to stay forever.

This book will show you how to accomplish your transformation from anxious to cool, nervous to calm. It will welcome you into a new sorority: a group that enjoys men, relationships, and illuminating adventures. What it won't do is secretly throw in little ways to meet a man. It won't gather a gaggle of friends to coo around your engagement ring, as if getting married were an accomplishment. It won't validate your anxiety about being single. I'm not here to tell you how to get married. Marriage is a wondrous thing, and if it's what you want, I wish you well in getting there. I have every confidence that you will—in your own sweet time and without discounting the amazing adventure that is your life, with or without a man in it. You're not a failure; you're not behind the curve. You're doing just fine.

SOMEDAY BUT NOT NOW

Marriage is a wondrous thing
For imps and gimps and mutts.
I knew a knock-kneed lady once
Who married a bowlegged klutz.

My father wrote this little poem on the occasion of his parents' twenty-fifth wedding anniversary. But for all his joking, he'd always tell anyone who'd listen that my mother was the best thing that ever happened to him. Even as a kid I knew that marriage didn't solve your problems—but it was a blessed stage nonetheless (even for the able-bodied).

My college roommate met her husband our senior year at the University of Pennsylvania. They spent every free minute together and after graduation both stayed on in Philadelphia. At age twenty-four they were married, and they are among the happiest-ever-after couples I know. I wore a peach bridesmaid dress to their wedding, with my hair severely sprayed into a rigid helmet around my head. Then, and many difficult times since, I have wondered: "What would my life be like if I had found The One at twenty-one? How much safer would the world seem if I knew who'd be walking beside me?"

In contrast to my roommate and her lifelong partner, my favorite aunt married once, at eighteen, and divorced shortly thereafter. For the rest of her life she dated an endless— at least as it appeared to my admiring eyes—collection of dashing men, including the masseur who could contort his body like a yogi and the comic book illustrator who inspired that gloriously rich, throaty laugh of hers. That she didn't marry again was considered a tragedy in my parents' home but to me made her bigger than life. She lived alone (alone!) and made her own money. She had lovers (lovers!) and a little Toyota she nicknamed Silver.

I imagine I lie somewhere in the middle of the continuum that runs from my roommate to my aunt. I'm thirty-three and someday I'll marry. Someday.

(My best friend once dragged me and my boyfriend at the time to a psychic who told me I'd marry someone "rich and powerful in New York." I pointed to my boyfriend, a great guy but neither rich nor powerful and said, "That's my boyfriend. He lives here in Washington, D.C." She shrugged, her fringed shawl falling to her elbows. "You'll move to New York?" she asked him. I questioned another of her predictions, and she turned on me. "Your whole life you're going to decide from a psychic?" she demanded, sounding suddenly more like a Jewish grandparent than a swami.)

MISTER RIGHT OR MISTERS RIGHT

In the wake of my broken engagement, I've given a lot of thought to when I might marry, and why, and to whom. Barbara Ehrenreich, tongue firmly in cheek, describes today's ideal husband:

> He should be a co-provider and a reliable financial partner; a co-conversationalist and sparkly dinner

companion, fully briefed by CNN. In the event of children, we expect he will further develop into a skilled co-parent with a repertoire of bedtime stories and remedies for runny noses. He should be prepared to jump into sweats and serve as a sturdy fitness partner, plus handling home repair; a husband who can't locate a fuse box is about as useful as one as one of those little plastic tool kits from Toys "R" Us. And since we are modern women, we have every right to think he will manage, in addition, to be a tireless and imaginative lover, supplying orgasms virtually on demand.[4]

Tall order isn't it? But I want all these things. Of course I know that no one person can be everything, so I'm a believer that the way to get it all is man by man, experience by experience. I believe the way to find out who I ultimately want to settle down with is by doing research in the field, experimenting, and trying out different types, each of whom may have a lot to offer but all of whom are quite different. He may be really smart or well-educated. He may be charming or gorgeous. He may have a wonderful sense of humor or want to accompany me on terrific adventures or appeal to my rebellious, artistic side or "just" be great in bed. Then when I do find a man I want to spend a lifetime with, I'll be able to weigh the importance of the pieces, the importance of sparkly conversation over sturdy athletics. Most important, I won't wonder what I missed, because I'll have had it all.

As I get to know myself better I understand more and more clearly that the journey is just as enriching and worthwhile as any destination. Back in my twenties and new to

Washington, I broke up with the boyfriend who had moved to town for me. A clunking washing machine of swirling, waterlogged emotions (anger, relief, and fear among them), I grabbed the beautiful chess set he had bought me and sent it tumbling to its death down the trash chute. Eight years later, just before I walked out of the home I shared with my fiancé, I dumped my jewelry box onto what had been our bed. I was aiming for both a "fair" and an unencumbered departure, but when I was over the pain of our parting, I began to miss a certain necklace. It was tiny, a thick silver "X," depicting a kiss. It wasn't at all the fact that he had bestowed it on me but rather how it felt nestled in the hollow of my neck, a burst of beauty on a fine string, that I missed.

Today I don't miss either guy, though I treasure the memories, the fun we had and the lessons dating them taught me about life and about myself. I'm far from hating either one, far from repressing those experiences.

But I still don't know how to play chess, and bare-necked, I miss that necklace. And I'm wondering, why did I toss the jewelry? That action has become kind of symbolic for me. Why disregard what these men, and others, have added to my life?

WHAT DO WOMEN WANT?

In *There Goes The Bride* I encouraged women to walk away from the wrong marriage. In fact statistics show that hundreds of thousands of women do break off their engagements every year. And after they've begun to understand the reasons they came so close to the wrong choice and have begun to recover from the inevitable shock and grief, the question for them becomes "What's next?"

The overwhelming chat room activity on my Web site (theregoesthebride.com) and the sustained attention to my first book from the media have shown that women are ready to think harder than they ever have about marriage. Hundreds of women have written to thank me for taking this message public: You don't win by landing the guy. You win by experiencing life and by loving yourself.

A middle-aged divorcee in Toronto wrote to me:

> I read your article today in the *National Post* about your book on almost marriages. I am so proud of you for doing this and I hope my own daughter will be able to have the strength to cope with all the emotions if ever she finds herself in the same situation.

At the same time, I was fielding letters like this one at my Web site:

> Dear Almost Bride:
> I find myself daydreaming that my boyfriend will do something wrong to give me a reason to break up with him. I have no reason. He is absolutely wonderful, we have the same interests, our families love each other, we are very compatible. Sometimes I feel there must be something wrong with me to feel doubtful about our relationship because technically it is perfect.
> I also find myself thinking more and more about packing up my stuff and moving back with my parents and starting a new life. I think about who I have

to call about address changes and how I'm going to set up my new room. All these signs seem to be pointing me in the direction of breaking up, but I can't seem to accept it because there is no reason. Are my feelings the reason?

I wrote back to her:

Why does there have to be a smoking gun? If you don't want it, you don't want it. Just because you can't write out the reasons in three lines or fewer doesn't make it any less so.

I think it goes back to the definition of "perfect." My perfect isn't going to be your perfect. And why should the fact that many things are great mean that this relationship is the one that knocks you over the head with the sheer fabulousness of it? In less flowery language: yes, just because you don't want to marry him *is* reason enough not to marry him.

Not every relationship is meant for marriage. Not every man is meant to be forever. As Pamela Paul, a journalist who lived through and then documented the painful phenomena of *starter marriages,* notes: "Many ascribe to the act of marriage transformative powers—[thinking] marriage can make a bad relationship good, transform an iffy obligation into solid commitment, turn a drug-abusing boyfriend into a corporate superstar, make a straying mate settle down."[5]

Yet so many of us buy into the hype—we've succeeded when and only when we've settled down. I used to wonder if I was wrong not to believe this and wrong to date without marriage in mind, but I don't anymore. And that's because I came within two weeks of marrying the wrong guy, and every day since I've thanked God we came to our senses. For a time after, I suffered intense grief and confusion about my life. All around me well-meaning people told me not to worry, that Mr. Right was out there and I'd find him and forget all about the ex-fiancé.

But even then that line of thinking irked me. I spent two years with my ex, and just because we didn't marry, those years weren't worth anything? I would argue that those were two of the most seminal years of my life. In them I learned what I want out of life, what I'm willing to compromise, and how compromising on some things can cause me physical pain.

DATING IS THE JOURNEY

I could even say that my ex-fiancé, "Mark," was the best thing that ever happened to me—just not in the way I originally thought he would be. Because if we hadn't been together, we wouldn't have broken up. Well-meaning people wouldn't have told me I'd forget all about him and find my true Mr. Right. And I wouldn't have realized that this is all part of the journey to me.

Thank you, Mark, for helping me realize how important it is to have this journey before I settle down.

Not everyone agrees with this approach. Writer Ann Roiphe says she likes Jane Austen's characters because of "the startling neatness and security of their destinies. They fall in love with the man whom history and class and tradition have chosen them for. . . . *This is the way it's supposed to be"* (Roiphe's emphasis).

"It doesn't seem stifling and moralistic anymore," Roiphe writes, "it seems civilized."[6] I don't buy it. I've never found comfort in being put into a box. When someone tells me I can't do something, I wonder what I'm missing. So I've gone against expectations. Now I'm living the life I always wanted, and my other single friends are too. We work hard at jobs we enjoy, travel, run marathons. But the one piece that hasn't fit is this: we profess to hate dating. We shake our heads at the mention of our ex-boyfriends, as if we can't believe we ever wasted time on the likes of them.

But we've been missing the point.

Dating is not supposed to be torture. It's not supposed to be a series of hoops, each one higher and smaller than the last, some of them ringed in fire, that we jump through to reach the nirvana of marriage. It may seem like the media, our mothers, and society are all in secret cahoots to make us panic if we're not married by a certain age. I'm here to tell you I've had enough. I don't treat being single like an emergency, and I'm no longer going to smile when my single friends contemplate dialing 911.

For kicks my friends and I watch so-called reality TV, which television producers assume means we'd like to skip the small talk and go straight to picking out the china. But life is nothing like the ABC hits *The Bachelor* and *The Bachelorette* or Fox's *Joe Millionaire.* And contrary to the opinion of TV producers, the reason women tune in is not to live vicariously through the chesty pinheads smiling pretty in the hopes of landing a gumball-sized diamond. It's to mock them. Studio suits may deem it "reality." Viewers consider it the ultimate escape from real life.

Take your time, that's what I say. And I'm not the first. Antoinette Brown Blackwell wrote:

> No grown up human being ought to rush blindly into this most intimate, most important, most enduring of human relations. . . . Let the young girl be instructed that, above her personal interests, her home, and social life, she is to have a great life purpose, as broad as the rights and interests of humanity. I say, let every young girl feel this, as much as every young man does. . . . Let her be taught that she ought not be married in her teens. Let her wait, as a young man does, if he's sensible, until she is twenty-five or thirty. She will then know how to choose properly, and probably she will not be deceived in her estimate of character; she will have had a certain life discipline, which will enable her to control her household matters with wise judgment, so that, while she is looking after her family, she may still keep her great life purpose, for which she was educated.[7]

And Blackwell wrote this in the late 1800s. (Think how old twenty-five or thirty was considered then!)

LET'S START A NEW MOVEMENT

There's an empowerment movement afoot that tells women to buy their own damn jewelry. I'm not against it, but I'm not one to turn down a man bearing gifts either. There's a group of women out there who say to hell with marriage. I shrug at that; I hope to someday spend the rest of my life with one man, but I'm not sitting home chaste and quiet until he shows up.

Many women have told me that they're tired of searching for a husband. My answer to that is: then don't. Instead I'm starting a movement. It's about living the life you want to live and enjoying the experiences, and the men, that come along. It's about appreciating everything you've learned from former boyfriends and eagerly anticipating the times with the ones to come. It's about not getting married just yet. It's about turning the volume on our anxieties down to low and, for today, enjoying Mr. Right Now.

I hope you'll join with me.

Rachel Safier

Chapter

Why You Can Afford to Wait

You can and should wait to marry, even though society's signals may keep making you feel you can't and shouldn't. But don't just take my word for it.

GOOD REASONS FOR WAITING

Here are some terrific reasons why you should wait and some expert opinions to back them up.

There Is No Man Shortage

In *Backlash,* Susan Faludi sounded off on the widely publicized 1986 Harvard-Yale study claiming that women face a dearth of men:

> A glance at past Census charts would . . . have dispelled the notion that the country was awash in a record glut of single women. The proportion of never-married women, about one in five, was lower than it had been at any time in the 20th century except the '50s, and even lower than the mid to late 19th century, when one in three women were unwed. . . . In fact, the only place where a "surplus" of unattached women could be said to exist in the '80s was in retirement communities. What was the median age of women who were living alone in 1986? Sixty-six years old.[1]

The same continues to hold true today: according to 2000 Census figures, the population of the United States is almost evenly split, with 49.1 percent men and 50.9 percent women. And we're getting married; according to the 2002 Census results, 50.5 percent of women aged fifteen and older are married; only slightly more men, 54.2 percent, are.[2] If those numbers seem low, thank God that most of us are waiting until we're at least out of high school to marry.

The Path We're on Both Helps Us Marry and Protects Us from Divorce

Even as Barbara Dafoe Whitehead, the author of *Why There Are No Good Men Left,* despairs of the "bleak" portrait of mating in this country, she admits that studies show that women with at least a B.A. degree are "more likely to marry and less likely to separate or divorce once they do marry than women with lower levels of educational attainment."[3]

Women Are Continuing to Marry

On the one hand, the TV news trumpets dire figures. On the other, how many of those damn bridesmaid dresses do you have hanging in your closet? Women are waiting—on purpose—but they are eventually crossing the threshold. "The marriage rate is the number of marriages per 1,000 unmarried women, [age] 15 and over, per year," Whitehead notes. "The marriage rate is not necessarily a measure of women's eventual marriage prospects, but many women take it to be."[4]

When we listen to our friends and not the evening news, the message is a relief. Faludi wrote of a 1986 national survey of women in their twenties and thirties in which 90 percent of the never-married women said "the reason they haven't [married] is that they haven't wanted to yet."[5] Today, more and more women are waiting to get married. If you think we single women are still in the closet, you haven't been watching *Sex and the City, Friends,* or even *Seinfeld* reruns. And Pamela Paul, author of *The Starter Marriage and the Future of Matrimony,* explains that even though we're marrying at a later age, we're "also marrying at an earlier stage in life . . . particularly given the fact that we mature earlier and live longer."[6] Rather than wait until we're completely financially steady—able to afford a marriage and a family—many of us marry before we own a home or have paid off our school loans.

Marriage Isn't All Wine and Roses

Yes, marriage is often wonderful. And it's often not. It's especially difficult if you marry the wrong guy because you jumped too fast. The people Pamela Paul interviewed thought that they were marrying for good, but marriage wasn't the finish line, and their for-good marriages became their first marriages.

Faludi recites a litany of maladies women in (I'm assuming unhappy) marriages suffer from, including "nervous breakdowns, nervousness, heart palpitations, and inertia. [And s]till other afflictions disproportionately plague married women: insomnia, trembling hands, dizzy spells, nightmares, hypochondria, passivity, agoraphobia and other phobias, unhappiness with their physical appearance, and overwhelming feelings of guilt and shame."[7] If you want to, you can even believe the various mental health data gathered on married men, married women, single men, and single women that find that the most happy are married men; the least happy, married women.

There Is No Proof That Marrying Young Is Better

Yes, youthful marriages do sometimes thrive. More often, however, they don't. Social conservatives offer many reasons to marry young—like having more children and growing with your mate—but none has been proven to keep a marriage intact. Pamela Paul writes that "[a]ccording to sociologist Larry Bumpass, 'The inverse relationship between age at marriage and the likelihood of marital disruption is among the strongest and most consistently documented in the literature.'. . . Even the [conservative] National Marriage Project conceded that there is no proof of greater success for marriages in the earlier twenties compared with those beginning in the late twenties and thirties. They conclude that a higher median age of marriage appears to have 'a strongly positive effect' on the institution as a whole."[8]

You Can't Hurry Love

You can hurry marriage, but that's not the same thing. When Fox first aired the show *Married by America*, which promised a deluxe wedding to couples America deemed right for each other, a local news program wanted to know my take. I told the reporter what I tell women over and over on my Web site: the reason to marry is to celebrate your commitment with family and friends.

A wedding doesn't make a commitment—marriage doesn't even cement it. If you're determined to run around on your partner, that little piece of paper isn't going to stop you. (Laura Kipnis, author of *Against Love: A Polemic,* doesn't think anything will stop us from cheating on each other. Her remedy: say to hell with marriage altogether.[9]) It's got to be in your heart. The wedding dress, the catered dinner, the flung-rice send-off are the fun extras, but they aren't the foundation. The foundation is love. Lois Brady, who writes vignettes about marrying and long-married couples for the *New York Times,* says, "There is nothing a woman can do to hurry love or to make it happen. Whenever anyone asks me about love, I always say, 'Wait for that feeling, wait, wait, wait. Wait with the patience of a Buddhist fly fisherman.'"[10] (That said, I loved *Married by America.* The timetable of a few weeks was too quick, but the series does show possibly starry-eyed women the issues that they'll have to tackle sooner or later—like outrageous in-laws and sexual appetites.)

Before You Can Know Someone Else
You've Got to Know You

You need to know yourself because it's necessary to your growth and because it's fun. Judith S. Wallerstein and Sandra Blakeslee, authors of *The Good Marriage*, are huge fans of the institution, but they understand the necessity of knowing yourself—whether or not you ever marry.

> To choose wisely in marriage a person first has to be able to stand alone. . . . To stand alone, you must feel that you have a choice and that you merit a choice, that somebody will choose you and that you will have the opportunity to choose in return.
>
> Standing alone does not mean just living in your own apartment after college. It does mean having a sense of self that allows you to go home alone from a party. It means being able to get through the night by yourself. It means not being driven by loneliness to make bad decisions about whom you invite into your apartment. In my experience, many wretched marriages have resulted from the fear of being alone even briefly.[11]

In *The Feminine Mystique*, Betty Friedan quotes psychiatrist Andras Angyal to explain the detriment of living vicariously through your partner:

> The most frequent manifestation of vicarious living is a particularly structured dependence on another per-

son, which is often mistaken for love. . . . [T]hese attachments are extremely possessive and tend to deprive the partner of a "life of his own." "Non-commitment" and "vicarious living," Angyal concludes, "can be understood as attempted solutions of the conflict between the impulse to grow and the fear of facing new situations," but though they may temporarily lessen the pressure, they do not actually resolve the problem; "their result, even if not their intent, is always an evasion of personal growth."[12]

And if you don't know life as a single, how can you choose the opposite? Peggy Orenstein, the author of *Flux*, points out that "if women can't see single life as a viable alternative with its own set of costs, rewards, and challenges, then they remain as controlled by marriage as previous generations, equally vulnerable to making choices negatively—out of fear instead of authentic desire."[13] And besides, as Friedan noted in 1963, "Love and children and home are good, but they are not the whole world, even if most of the words now written for women pretend they are. Why should women accept this picture of a half-life, instead of a share in the whole of human destiny?"[14]

Education Leads to Success, Even in Marriage

There is no better way to get to know yourself and to succeed in whatever life you build than by getting a solid education. In 1952, Simone de Beauvoir despaired of putting marriage above school:

Parents still raise their daughters with a view to marriage rather than to furthering her personal development; she sees so many advantages in it that she herself wishes for it; the result is that she is often less specially trained, less solidly grounded than her brothers, she is less deeply involved in her profession. In this way, she dooms herself to remain in its lower levels, to be inferior; and the vicious circle is formed: this professional inferiority reinforces her desire to find a husband.[15]

Fast-forward about fifty years, and Beauvoir's view is backed up by the reviewers at Princeton University who shot down "Too Late for Prince Charming," that cockamamie *Newsweek* story that said a never-married thirty-five-year-old woman had a mere 5 percent chance of ever marrying. The Princeton University study concluded, "marriage levels will be highest for those women who are, in theory, most able to live well alone—the most highly educated."[16]

Education is also "divorce insurance," as Whitehead points out.[17] If our marriage fails, we've got the skills to support ourselves. As Erica Jong says, a feminist is "a woman who assures self-dependence as a basic condition of her life."[18] And with the knowledge of the big world out there that education gives, we're less likely to settle for the first guy who comes along.

BAD REASONS FOR RUSHING AHEAD

Many of us have been subjected to a lot of propaganda and paranoia about why we should get married as soon as possible. So here are some common admonitions and popular myths that may sound familiar and must be debunked.

You Have to Have Babies
When You're Really Young

Not necessarily—your years for having babies aren't limited to your twenties, not even absolutely to your thirties. The fact is you can have babies for longer than you used to. And if you enter a marriage just to have babies, what are the chances of that marriage lasting? And how can that be good for your kids? If you want children so badly, why not forgo the trappings of marriage and just have them?

You're Not Really an Adult Until You Marry

That's the belief our mothers push on us, right? Even pundit psychologist Erik Erikson posited that "the formation of romantic love attachments [is] the defining developmental task for young people."[19] And in the race for adulthood, Whitehead believes that women have "time to find a loving mate, but not a lot of time to waste on the other kind. It's important to avoid drift and delay."[20] But this kind of thinking looks at love and life like a game, something that can be won or cruelly lost.

Pop quiz. One woman finishes college with a ring on her finger. She and her fiancé marry soon after. A second woman finishes college with only a degree. The first woman endures a painfully mismatched union as she and her youthful sweetheart grow up and away from each other. The second woman dates and works and grows up too. The first woman divorces after fifteen or twenty long years. The second woman lives most of her adult life "alone," only meeting the man she wants to settle down with in her mid-forties, the same age at which the first woman divorces her husband. Who won?

And when are you really an adult anyway? Is it when you lose your virginity? When you no longer take money from your parents? When you marry? When you own a home? When you have children? When your own parents die? When you publish your first book? When a national newspaper reviews that book and the headline trumpets, "But She's Not Bitter!"[21] (I certainly aged a decade or so on reading that.)

You Don't Have Time to Both Work Hard and Find a Husband

There's an idea that if you find love early you can go on to pursue your other goals, knowing you've got the marriage one out of the way. This is tied up with the feeling that it's every man for himself; society isn't helping, so you've got a second job finding love.

So many of the women I have interviewed felt strong emotions ranging from guilt to clinical depression on the breakup of their engagements—regardless of whether they were the ones who called it off, why it was called it off, or whether one party was at fault. Many of them expressed sorrow that they had given their exes years of their lives. But as Pepper Schwartz, author of *Everything You Know About Love and Sex Is Wrong*, says: "You do need to 'waste' time. You do need to assume that you don't always know what you like and who is worth knowing."[22]

Men Are Intimidated by Too Much Achievement

Obviously you want to couple with a man who wants a razor-sharp, successful woman. Don't lean on the legend that you will repulse men by your high-powered career and unstoppable ambition in order to justify career laziness. This belief may once have served you well. In the past, says Rosalind Miles, in *The Women's History of the World,* schooling women provided "every chance of direct economic disadvantage, since an educated woman could so easily price herself out of the marriage market. . . . The risk of learning was that it promoted a woman beyond her 'place.'"[23]

Times have changed. Of course most men aren't going to want a woman who is a braggart about her achievements, just as most of us wouldn't want a man who is that way. But the real truth today is that a smart woman doesn't scare off men. I mean, come on. When a girlfriend tells me that a date didn't call her again because he was "intimidated" by her, I think: "No, honey, he just didn't like you. Big brains and all."

The World Looks Differently at a Wife

In *A History of the Wife,* Marilyn Yalom recalls the time when ". . .women wore the title 'wife' like a badge of honor. To be a parson's wife, a baker's wife, a doctor's wife told the world loudly and clearly that one had fulfilled one's 'natural' destiny. It spoke for legitimacy and protection in a world that was proverbially unkind to spinsters. Whether one was happily married or not, the wedding ring, in and of itself, was a measure of female worth."[24]

When your mom harangues you, however, I promise it's not about legitimacy and protection—it's about grandchildren! We may think tongues are wagging, but there are so many choices for women today—single, married, divorced, remarried, lesbian with a steady lover, single mom, and so on and so forth—that it's just impossible to be pigeonholed ever again.

The Media's Got Your Number

Back in the 1960s, Mary Tyler Moore made waves by starring in the first TV show that portrayed—and starred!—an unmarried, professional woman. Our options have come a long way since then (remember when Rachel, on *Friends*, turned down Joey's proposal when she got pregnant by Ross, saying it wasn't a husband she was looking for?). And yet by and large TV shows still assume that our preference is for images of the Perfect Day (our wedding day of course) and the Perfect Guy. In TV-land unmarried women are so lonely they probably bay at the moon when the cameras aren't aimed at them (see *Ally McBeal*) and are lining up to meet a producer-picked bachelor. To get on with your life, you need to turn off the television and live it.

Literature's got your number too: from Cinderella to the popular genre of Chick Lit, women worry about living a partnerless life. So much for reading for relaxation. (Yoga, anyone?)

Repeat after me: "I will *wait* to marry. I will *wait* to marry." Now let's deconstruct the fiction surrounding the man you will marry someday. I don't mean to burst all your bubbles in one day, but Mr. Right is a myth.

Chapter

2

Don't Wait For Mr. Right

All my single girlfriends are waiting for Mr. Right.

Personally, I picture someone tall, with thick, black hair and deep blue eyes.

Deep as the ocean even.

Maybe he's standing on a cliff.

No, no cliff: he's wearing a suit, and he's striding purposefully. That detail is important to me: he's got somewhere to go.

Why are we so obsessive about this eternal search for someone perfect? Let's take a look at this phenomenon and see if there's any way to break the habit.

HISTORICAL ROOTS OF THE GREAT SEARCH

Anna Rosner of the University of Toronto wrote her thesis on the consequences for women who chose not to marry, as they were shown in French literature of the seventeenth and eighteenth centuries. I sought her out to help me understand the roots of our interest in "happily ever after." Rosner explained to me that the concept of a Mr. Right has changed over the years and is subjective, depending on the author's perspective. In French literature of the 1600s, authors' bent was Christianity, and Mr. Right was either the man your father had chosen for you, or God—because one of women's few alternatives to the institution of marriage was the nunnery. (I would just like to point out that if I had let my father choose, I would be married right now to a very sweet, very boring, small New York attorney I never even dated. I yawn to think of it.)

In much of early literature, Mr. Right is a tool to teach women their appropriate, submissive place in society; as such, he's chosen by a woman's family or society. In literature powered by authors with a more feminist bent, Mr. Right is chosen by the female character, and he *allows* her freedom. Mr. Right is sometimes even a gallant, platonic love and thus a thoughtful turning away from the strictures of marriage.

"As a general rule," Rosner says, "female authors of the eighteenth century often privilege platonic space and friendship over marriage, because the institution was so oppressive and discriminatory; women had very few rights within the marriage bounds." In other words, marriage roles were narrowly defined. Women either accepted the rules or became spinsters or nuns. There were no single, dating women. And any women who aspired to that role were beaten back: "The 'good' woman is subtle, asexual, lustless, controlled, God-fearing, and a good mother," Rosner found. "The 'bad' woman is sexual, dissatisfied, an unnatural mother or a woman who refuses marriage or motherhood; perhaps she laughs too loud. . . . The typical female trajectory will lead to one of two possibilities: early death or, eventually, marriage."[1] (I considered titling *Mr. Right Now* as *Early Death or Eventually Marriage* instead. Has a nice ring to it, no?)

In Flaubert's *Madame Bovary,* for example, the heroine, Emma, believes she's marrying for love but then realizes that although her husband is kindhearted, he's frankly rather dull. Rosner translates from the original French: "Before she married, she believed in her love; but since the happiness that should have resulted from this love did not come, she must have been mistaken, she thought. And Emma wondered what exactly was meant in life by the words *happiness, passion* and *ecstasy,* which had seemed so beautiful in books." Emma tries again, despite her suspicion that the love she seeks exists only in fiction, searches for love outside of marriage, and finally meets Mr. Wrong; he abandons her and she commits suicide.

SEARCHING FOR PERFECTION

Sure, these frightening, cautionary tales from literature might not seem to apply directly to us today, but why then do we women stubbornly keep up our valiant search for fairy tale perfection? The definition of Mr. Right has changed over the years—along with women's options—but we still hold on to a fantasy man who doesn't exist. Are we really that much wiser or freer than Emma? We refuse to be happy with our relationships or ourselves until we find Mr. Right, that paragon of perfection we have built up in our minds.

Jeffry Larson, author of *Should We Stay Together*, takes issue with the myth that says, "Until a person finds the perfect person to marry . . . she should not be satisfied."[2]

> If you believe there is the perfect partner for you somewhere out there, you will be likely to engage in short-term "rating relationships" in order to more quickly identify if a person is Mr. or Miss Perfect. After all, who wants to waste their time dating someone with whom there is no future? Instead of getting to know your dates and relating to them, you will evaluate and *rate them*—prematurely. You will then develop a pattern of multiple short-term relationships, which lead to frustration, disappointment, and disillusionment for both you and your dating partners. The pointlessness of this belief is further amplified by the fact that people change over time. The person who appeared perfect at the beginning of the relationship will inevitably appear imperfect later.[3]

Larson and I both believe you shouldn't look for a perfect partner. But we differ on the value of short-term relationships. That said, I agree that the mind-set of "rating" each person you're with is not a good idea. This book is not about having "rating relationships in order to more quickly identify Mr. or Miss Perfect." It's about enjoying and relishing each Mister you meet, about appreciating him for who he is, and through him, learning more about yourself.

When you look at it that way, how can short-term dating *not* be crucial? What could be more important than getting to know yourself? Why shouldn't we spend our youth living life, enjoying dating, and taking the scenic route? Don't look at each date as possibly The One—because when he's not, as is usually the case, you're going to feel frustrated and disillusioned, as Larson says. Instead, look at dating—at life, really—as an adventure.

I bought a refrigerator magnet in the flower district of Amsterdam that I cherish. It shows the open road and below the picture is written: "Life is short, but it's wide." Don't focus on the end, which is always sooner than we'd like. Focus instead on the oceans of space to the left and to the right of you.

WANTING SAFETY AND STABILITY

According to Deborah Shelkrot Permut, a therapist in Washington, D.C., women consider finding Mr. Right the way to achieve a simple, age-old goal: safety and stability. Women often strongly want to be married and to have a family, and Mr. Right seems the way to get there.

Permut counsels clients against choosing a man who is perfect on paper, and I can completely relate. In therapy sought after the breakup of my engagement, I began to realize that "Mark" was perfect in theory but nothing that I was looking for. That realization opened up a Pandora's box—Why had I been seduced by society's ideas of "perfect" rather than being in touch with my own? Figuring out the answer to that has been the key to my happiness today.

And I'm doing my best to spread that gospel.

I received this letter on my Web site:

I'm currently in a very serious relationship with my boyfriend, Milton. We've been living together for almost a year, dating for more than two. About a month ago I was overwhelmed with feelings of doubt and left to seek refuge at my parent's home. I've been here ever since trying to get some clarity about my feelings and follow my heart. I'm not sure I know how to do that.

There was no trigger or event that led up to this, only feelings in my stomach that something was not quite right. How do you determine if those feelings are truly feelings of doubt or some deeper psychological issue within you (that is, I'm not happy with myself)? I don't feel like going back to our apartment to be with him, but I'm so scared to be without him.

Though it would have been quick, and might have been what she wanted to hear, I couldn't tell the writer of this letter to just keep walking. What I could do—and did do—was help her explore those feelings. What is happiness? Where does Milton fit in?

Today women are always asking me what insights I've gained. What do I do now, in the wake of a failed engagement, to help myself find Mr. Right? I have two answers. There is no Mr. Right. And I date. I date a lot. I allow myself to be attracted to a man, even when he's blindingly, obviously, not the man I want to build a life with. If he's adventurous, dangerous, smart, or a sexy bright light I'm attracted to like a moth, I'll approach. Life is about fun and stimulation and experience. He can be my Mr. Almost; he doesn't have to be my Mr. Everything.

Some people find this approach unnerving. What about having kids? What about dating exhaustion? What about wasting time? Ah, that's the question. That's the hidden fear. Clients of Eric Levin, a Philadelphia therapist specializing in dating, are always bringing that one up. "People rush in because they are getting older and are afraid of not meeting someone else, afraid time is passing," Levin says. What they don't stop to realize is that "the real time killer is bad relationships, not prolonged nonexclusive dating. Once you're on the 'monogamy train,' a relationship is hard to break off, even when the writing is well on the wall. You *could* have been dating him and other people [instead of rushing to marry him]. People who marry after two years and then divorce ten years and two kids later—*that's* a time waster, not two months of nonexclusive dating."

Ah, but here's the Greek chorus, anxious and melancholy, wringing their hands behind me:

> But if he's Mr. Right,
> Shouldn't he be The One,
> The Only One?

THE DANGERS OF THE BIG SEARCH

When you stop to think about it, the idea of Mr. Right is nothing short of dangerous. If he's perfect, everything he believes must be too (so what if you think differently). And your world becomes smaller; bit by bit he blocks the sun. When clients tell Deborah Permut that they despair of finding

Mr. Right, however hard they look, her thought process (expressed to her clients in myriad ways) goes something like this:

Is a man really what she's looking for?
If it is, is that the right direction to look for what she needs?
If it is, what's her definition of Mr. Right?

Baltimore therapist Marci Drimer is annoyed with our parents, society, the media, and even fairy tales for perpetuating the myth of Mr. Right. "Women are raised to believe in the prince rescuing the princess," she laments. She tells clients to forget about looking for Prince Charming. Not because she believes the old saw that when you're comfortable and happy with yourself the right guy will come along but because she thinks you'll actually be attracted to the right guy. She also stresses that it's only when you are your "honest, genuine, and true self" that you're open to welcoming the right person in. And it's only when you're on solid footing that you can realize that having someone in your life romantically "makes it that much better, but it doesn't *make* you happy."

Drimer warns against looking for the "heart-pounding, flowers and candy person"—an essential piece of fiction for Mr. Right devotees. (My tall, black-haired, blue-eyed gentleman has his hands full of tulips; he's probably striding purposefully toward me to present them.) Clients often tell her that if they're not madly in love after the first date, the guy's all wrong.

Permut has seen clients "choosing and foreclosing" on the

dating experience too soon. If they believe they've found Mr. Right (and some women are willing and eager to bend over backward to make a man look perfect), women will choose not to date others. There is danger in "focusing on him and not having enough other experiences," Permut says. "Not just ones to decide who is your Mr. Right but ones to help you learn about yourself and become more of yourself." In focusing on one person and proclaiming him perfect, a woman "gives up all her power, losing her self."

I'm a huge fan of marrying later to prevent such loss of self, but Permut doesn't believe it's necessarily that simple. Rather, maturity is demonstrated in "openness to experience and to learning about oneself. Focusing on finding a partner instead of learning about oneself is what keeps one from developing as a person." Not having enough experiences would be one of the things that cause a woman to be subsumed by her partner. Her psychological makeup and history are others. Age is another. In the end it's "what we do with our experiences and what we learn from them," Permut counsels. "How fearful are we about being out in the world, about learning about ourselves? How dependent do we feel?"

In the Acknowledgments, I mention a number of therapists whom I've talked to about the ideas examined in this book. I've included their opinions here and throughout this book so your college-trained brain can accept the merit of these ideas academically. At the same time, *this* expert on life is encouraging you to throw out your antiquated ideas of the future. The world is a smorgasbord of Misters to be sampled. Forget about Mr. Right; don't think about forever.

And jump in.

This book is all about the joy of jumping in, moving on, and jumping in again. Life is one big diving board, and dating is a swimming pool. Come on in—the water's great. The world is full of Misters for you to remember and enjoy.

Let's start with everybody's first—Mr. Puppy Love.

Chapter

3

Mr. Puppy Love

In fifth-grade social studies class one day, I was chosen to lead a presentation by a group of four students, and I gave a brief introduction before each of my classmates spoke. A sandy-haired boy with big brown eyes was feeling shy that day, so for his introduction I said, "And lastly, Sammy, who is currently under his desk."

And then sometime between ages ten and sixteen, Sammy came out from under his desk and blossomed—in my eyes at least—and I fell for Mr. Puppy Love.

We've all been there. And unlike some of our other relationships along the highway, this is one we all remember fondly. When I had secured my precious driver's license, I would point the car toward Sammy's neighborhood to "run errands." And once there, I would call his house to say I happened to be in the area and was he around?

I talked about him with my friends, who talked about their own crushes. I look at him now and feel nothing, but when I was sixteen, the sound of his name made me light up. We spent hours on the phone and some of the best nights of my life (I've lived a little since then) lying on the hood of his car, with Peter Gabriel's *So* cranked up loud. My father said I couldn't sleep over at his house, so we'd stay up all night instead, and I'd drive home at dawn, feeling only mildly guilty.

He made a couple of passes at me, but scared kid that I was, I kept pushing back, so the relationship never crossed the line from intense flirtation. I remember sitting close to him, on a moss-green rocking couch on his back porch, with his arm around me, and getting up every fifteen minutes to check my hair in the bathroom mirror. I remember the excitement of his looking at me with desire, of our long, soulful hugs before we parted. Embarrassed now, I remember all those stupid errands run in his neighborhood that could have easily been run in mine (if they even needed to be run at all). He was really just your average guy, but I sure didn't know it.

And at the time there was nothing like it. Close your eyes and remember your Mr. Puppy Love. Was he an across-the-classroom crush who never knew you existed? Some teen pop star, whose face stared down at you lovingly from the poster above your bed? An otherwise platonic friend you secretly fantasized about? An older brother's best friend? A friend of mine named Carolyn remembers her Mr. Puppy Love as "dreamy! A tall, quiet basketball player at my high school. I really didn't know him very well at all but I thought he was the cutest!"

We were truly puppies in love, bounding after the objects of our affection, then hiding in the shadows to watch them. We showed ourselves to be incredible doofuses. If we displayed the same behavior in adulthood that we did with our first crush, we'd be considered unstable stalkers:

> Every time I saw him, I flipped out, even when I was only a few feet away.
>
> —Hilary

> I actually would call his answering machine and see if he kept my messages or just deleted them (I knew he kept the messages that were important to him).
>
> —Billie

> I was not absent for a single day during the eighth grade. I wouldn't miss a day of Andy Levine if I were bleeding from my eyes.
>
> —Jane

WHY WE'RE WALKING DOWN MEMORY LANE

Remember your first crush? Your first boyfriend? The first time you fell in love? (Everyone say, "Ah . . .") Like your experiences with Mr. Dangerous and Mr. Sex, which we'll look at soon, these first experiences help make up your grand adventure. These Misters—the ones you've had so far, the ones to come—are all worth the trip. You may think, "Well, sure, my time with Mr. Puppy Love was fun while it lasted. But it's over, done with, kaput, and here I am adrift in the sea of singlehood. Why do you have to remind me of what I had? And how does enjoying staring at Andy Levine in fifth-grade science class translate into enjoying danger or sex?"

First, if you really speak this way, I suggest you look into a career with Hallmark.

Second, that's the beauty of this movement. Not everything is what it seems—it's most often deeper and cooler (and you can be too). Later in this book I'll explain why Mr. Dangerous and Mr. Sex and all the other Misters should be considered. For now, let me explain why Mr. Puppy Love meant more than staring at Andy Levine (cute as he was).

THE TRUE MEANING OF PUPPY LOVE

We don't just fall for Mr. Puppy Love. We stumble and hurtle headlong into his locker while trying to stroll nonchalantly past him. What is it about Mr. Puppy Love that elicits such strong passion?

Turns out it's not much. When asked why they liked him, the women I talked to were pretty vague, saying things like, "I just thought he was cute and tall—I didn't know much more about him," or, "I thought he was out of my league," or in the case of Ingrid, whose puppy love story is told later in this chapter, "He was a hero."

Puppy love is funny that way. It's not so much about who he really is or how you are together but what he elicits in you. Dahlia's Mr. Puppy Love was a few grades ahead in high school and sent her flowers a few times before they even talked. Dahlia was conservative in her pastel Merona sweaters and straight hair that hung down her back. Rob looked like he never brushed his curly mane, and he wore a long, over-sized men's coat that swept the floor as he walked past. His rebelliousness appealed to her. Hope tried on adult desire by falling for a boy who "was everything that you dreamed about when you were young. Tall, dark, handsome, intelli-gent, athletic . . . you name it."

Most women interviewed had coveted older boys, maybe casting them in the role of comforter and protector. In Ingrid's case her puppy love literally saved a life:

> Kurt was tall, handsome, funny, and well-liked by everyone who met him. He was four years older than me. I developed a huge crush on him the summer I was ten. We were waterskiing—my two brothers, Kurt and his sister, two of our friends, and me. My younger brother fell and got wedged under a dock. Kurt dove off the boat, which was going at full throttle, swam under the dock and rescued him. That was it for me—I was done. I kept that crush on him for five years.

The joy of puppy love isn't like the joys of later relation-ships. It's not "adult"—it's not about caring strongly for the welfare of someone who cares strongly back. It's not about laughing together or tumbling into bed. Rather, it's the first time you allow yourself to experiment with a full-scale crush and see how it feels. It's about your own private pleasure; Mr. Puppy Love himself has very little to do with it.

"I loved that slightly sick-in-the-stomach feeling," one woman remembers. "It is so exciting," says another. "You have that sixth-grade feeling. Everything feels wonderful and you just can't beat it with a stick!" Mr. Puppy Love is all about the thrill of the other—the jolt you get when you hear his name, the sudden lightheadedness you feel as he walks by.

And then you wake from the dream. "There isn't a physical relationship," Billie says. "You feel your heart sink when the object of your affection starts to mention others or starts dating someone else." The agony is that sudden reality—the feelings are self-generated, and eventually you're going to want someone else in on the pleasure. "It's always just out of your reach," says Hope. "I watched him start dating my older cousin," Ingrid says. "They eventually married."

We all grow up and away from puppy love. (Well, we should, but more on that in a minute.) When we're mature enough, we step back from the frame and let someone else into the picture. Billie fell in puppy love a number of times, but then she started to realize there was more than mooning to romance. "I think I am the queen of these one-sided relationships," she explains. "Sometimes it is easier to love from afar, but it is not as rewarding as a real relationship. I learned to look for a relationship where somebody feels the same way I feel about him."

Ingrid, whose crush saved her brother's life, continues to carry a torch for the best pieces of her puppy love. "I still look for humor and I still swoon at the slightest gesture of bravery or chivalry," she realizes.

IT'S ALL ABOUT ME

Puppy love is about infatuation. It really doesn't have anything to do with true love or with deep feelings and the desire to understand the other's personality that go along with that emotion. And it's wonderful. The girl is in the driver's seat—and there are no passengers. Puppy love doesn't have anything to do with the object of the "love." It is about what is going on with the girl, what she is excited about, what is triggered in her.

Women often believe that their first big crush means that they will ultimately partner with someone like Mr. Puppy Love or that he is their true destiny. However, therapist Deborah Shelkrot Permut explains that the beauty of this crush is not that Mr. Puppy Love is your destiny, it's that you were able, for a while at least, to enjoy a self-centered sensation, a fever, an internalized passion unrelated to the reality of someone else.

It's worth it not just to remember Mr. Puppy Love fondly but to recapture your actual feelings about the guy you couldn't have. Remember how you felt when you gazed up at the David Cassidy or Matt Dylan posters on your walls? Not too long ago I was rustling through the 1980s fashions stowed in my childhood closet, and I looked up and noticed a Ralph Macchio poster still hanging there too. I couldn't help the feeling that spread through my chest. It wasn't about sex; it was more about being very awake, very attuned to those eyes, those lips. And it wasn't about meeting Ralph Macchio. That's something a friend of mine also discovered about crushes. She had incurable puppy love for Adam Ant and managed to get tickets to see him on *Saturday Night Live.* As he passed through the gauntlet of eager autograph seekers, he stopped right in front of her. And she froze. Her bedroom in the suburbs was covered with pictures of him, she blasted his records, but when he was *right there,* in all his purple-jacket-with-the-epaulets-on-the-sleeves glory, she couldn't think of a single thing to say.

I loved Sammy from afar through high school but lost him (if I had ever had him) to a statuesque, strawberry-blond runner. (Then he lost her to her old boyfriend, and the cycle goes on). We continued to flirt, to push and pull for years. Then finally, in a burst of adulthood, I realized I was fed up. I was feeling pretty rootless, and Sammy suggested I move out West, where he and a few of our high school friends had migrated. I thought he was making overtures I was now mature enough to respond to. But when I got to his house, he acted strangely, keeping his distance, choosing to stay in when the rest of us went out on the town. Later that night he told me he didn't feel "it." I looked him in the eye and said: "This stops right here, right now. We're friends, without innuendo." He looked pretty scared, but probably less because I was closing the door on us and more because he'd always seen me as floating lightly within the aura of his Sammyesque charms.

I stalked out, took a good long walk up and down San Francisco's killer hills, and shook him off. I thought for a long time that Sammy was a jerk. Now I think it's just a shock to any woman when Mr. Puppy Love loses his aura.

My friend went speechless in the presence of Adam Ant because her crush was all about that aura. And then the older and more experienced we get, the less the aura matters and the more dating starts to feel like a doctor's visit, with women too often taking the relationship's pulse or urging it to take better care of itself, plumping it up or slimming it down. What we can get from Mr. Puppy Love is the Zen of acceptance. "Sammy: Ah." That simple. I want to remember that feeling, use it in the future. That feeling of puppy love and the pure, unadulterated moment.

I once told a boyfriend our being together wasn't working out because we were standing still and relationships needed momentum. I was young and stupid. This isn't the Indy 500 we're dealing with.

Which is not to say that you want all Mr. Puppy Love all the time. When puppy love—feelings minus the actual other person—carries over into adulthood, infatuation becomes the more dangerous obsession. According to Baltimore therapist Marci Drimer, obsession can downright interfere with life. Drimer has had clients who "call a zillion times a day, not able to concentrate on work, not able to pay attention to their kids because they're gabbing on the phone with friends about the boyfriend, they're getting distracted, letting bills slide."

In other words, full-blown puppy love's not so cute later in life.

Ah, but when you're a kid . . .

Mr. Puppy Love helps us get used to the idea of romance without going out on a limb and being vulnerable to someone else. He's perfect for the young and the uninitiated. When you're ready to kiss a boy and not just your pillow, there's Mr. First Boyfriend.

Been There, Learned This

So you wouldn't want all your romances to be puppy love, but some qualities of this first experience with idealized romance are wonderful and can be preserved in later, more mature relationships. For example, as you experience a current romance, see if you can . . .

o Hearken back to the time when the thrill was in the chase, not the capture. It wasn't about getting his number, it was about getting a smile.

o Concentrate on the feelings. The rush when you think of him, the tingle when his leg brushes yours, the sheer joy of hearing his voice on the other end of the phone.

o Remember that it's all about the trip. The ride stops and you'll step off—all in one piece and gloriously dizzy.

A THERAPIST WEIGHS IN

Puppy love is what is known as *neurotic excitement*, which means that the feeling is about the woman's issues, her unresolved conflicts, and how the guy fits into them.
—Deborah Shelkrot Permut, LCSW, Psy.D.
Washington, D.C.

Check Yourself Quiz
IS HE JUST MR. PUPPY LOVE?

Answer "Yes" or "No" to each question. Then use the scoring section to check whether Mr. Puppy Love is for you.

_____ 1. He makes me laugh.

_____ 2. I know where he lives, but I'm not sure he knows where I do.

_____ 3. We've kissed.

_____ 4. When I hear his voice, my heart starts thumping.

_____ 5. He's met my folks.

_____ 6. He's dating someone else.

_____ 7. He knows what color my eyes are.

_____ 8. I'd approach him, but my tongue gets all knotted up.

_____ 9. I'd describe him as "dreamy."

_____ 10. He's taking up a lot of space in my diary.

SCORING

1.	Yes: 0	No: 1		6.	Yes: 1	No: 0
2.	Yes: 1	No: 0		7.	Yes: 0	No: 1
3.	Yes: 0	No: 1		8.	Yes: 1	No: 0
4.	Yes: 1	No: 0		9.	Yes: 1	No: 0
5.	Yes: 0	No: 1		10.	Yes: 1	No: 0

0–5   He's not just a crush.

6–7   He could just be Mr. Puppy Love. If that's what you'd like him to be, call his house a few times and hang up when he answers.

8–10   Stand back and enjoy the show. He's only Mr. Puppy Love, but sometimes that's all you need.

WE MEET AGAIN

Nancy Kalish went looking for lost love and found it. Her Lost Love Project, a study of 1,500 people who attempted a romantic reunion with a puppy love or young love, found that 72 percent of the couples who found each other stayed together. So maybe when we say good-bye to our puppy loves we should really be saying, "See you later!"

Kalish, N. *Lost and Found Lovers: Facts and Fantasies of Rekindled Romances*. New York: Morrow, 1997.

MR. PUPPIEST LOVE: RALPH MACCHIO

I fell hard and fast for Ralph Macchio when I saw *The Outsiders*. The two thoughts drumming in my head were, "Why won't his momma take care of him?" and, "Can I?" We may all fall in puppy love with him, but would you want to date Ralph Macchio, the puppiest of them all?

PROS

○ He cleans a mean fence. ("Wax on. Wax off.")
○ You can save him from going "bad." (Remember him as the borderline thuggish teen on *Eight Is Enough*? His love for Abby's niece and the Bradford family's love for him brought him over to the good side.)
○ He's just dreamy in that jean jacket with the collar turned up. Sigh.

CONS

○ You could knock him over with a feather.
○ Everybody thinks of him as fifteen, but he's (gulp) in his forties.
○ His karate mentor, Mr. Miyagi, is part of the bargain.

Chapter

4

Mr. First Boyfriend

Do you remember your first boyfriend?

> Five feet eight inches tall. Glasses. Smart. Runner. Good at crisis management. Our personalities fit each other incredibly well and we were attracted to each other. He is still one of my best friends.
> —*Ingrid*

> Wow, he was great. He always did things for me. He was always around for me. Walked me places. Wrote me notes. He was sensitive (I think I discovered why on this one: he turned out to be gay).
> —*Eloise*

He was seventeen and got his driver's license before me. He had blond hair and brown eyes. He was a little chubby, but again a nice, polite guy. His face turned red easily when he got embarrassed. He was also athletic—a good tennis player. I had my first kiss with him.

—Mandy

I still have a photograph of Michael, taken the time we first met in our freshman year at Penn. He's lanky and long, dark and smiling, with a do-rag wrapped around his thick black hair. He was a swimmer, and I can remember standing in the library stairwell dreamily thinking about the way his torso formed a triangle from his broad shoulders to his small waist.

Michael and I had nothing in common besides finding each other attractive. He was wealthy, shallow, liked to toke with his friends, and spoke poorly of his mother. His idea of a good time involved spending a great deal of money—he took me to see *A Chorus Line* on Broadway, a pretty expensive date for an eighteen-year-old. He talked about a career in banking because he wanted to make piles of money. I can't remember a single deep conversation between us, though I do remember singing Cat Stevens's songs all the way home during a late-night train ride. When we reached our stop, a passenger thanked us for the entertainment.

I went off for the summer with friends to a house on Cape Cod. Between seating people in much coveted booths in my bust-hugging "Colonial" uniform at my hostess job, I wrote Michael long, deeply felt letters about life and love and the future—mine, not his. I'm not sure I even mailed them; even then I could imagine him scanning them quickly for the parts about him.

THE ROLE OF MR. FIRST BOYFRIEND

After the thrill of Mr. Puppy Love wore thin, we all were ready for Mr. First Boyfriend. He wasn't perfect for us (who is?), but he's part of our history.

Before I left town for the summer, Michael wanted to go out every night. He was working in a hip downtown store and spent his paycheck on clothes. I wanted to spend some nights with other friends or even alone, and Michael balked. To him a romance meant plenty of proximity. It also meant love: he ended every phone call telling me he loved me. I never returned the sentiment. And it meant sex; when I refused to go that far, he left me. I cried with this new kind of pain for one night and felt flattened for another week or two. I remember moping around my mother's house in a fluffy pink bathrobe.

Oh, sure, my grief ended after some time of knocking around in my bathrobe, fingering decomposing Kleenex in the pockets. After all, the relationship never got much more advanced than a few months of superficial bliss over being wanted.

THE JOY OF SHOWING

It's a tautology—a meaningless repetition of an idea, "chasing your tail," as my sixth-grade English teacher, Mrs. Santos, used to say. A big piece of the appeal of having a boyfriend is . . . having a boyfriend. Where Mr. Puppy Love is admiration from afar, Mr. First Boyfriend is admiration from closer in, but mostly just so you can tell friends about it. As you did with Mr. Puppy Love, you're learning a great deal about yourself in the process. And here the process includes actual touching.

> It was fun to be a couple; to have the attention. I got to finally do the "couple" things I had seen my friends do. Go out on dates to the movies. Buy a Christmas present for "my boyfriend." On Valentine's Day I actually had a valentine for the first time.
> —*Billie*

> The best part of it was hearing my friends say, "Nancy's boyfriend."
> —*Nancy*

> I just loved telling people, "I have a boyfriend, and he's older and he's popular and he drives."
> —*Vera*

With Mr. First Boyfriend, we tell the world we're attractive and coveted, that we're not little girls anymore. And we're trying to convince ourselves of the same. We're declaring a new level of maturity: we have moved beyond wanting someone from afar to wanting him up close. Polly fondly remembers "the hand-holding and marathon phone conversations. We used to sleep with our phones in bed and talk for hours. It was so very sweet and innocent." But a big piece of the first boyfriend experience also is discovering—and acting on—our lust.

What was the joy of your first boyfriend?

He was the first person that spoke to and touched me like I was a woman. As much as I resisted him—and as little touching as I returned—this touching was my first foray into that exciting and sensual world of adulthood.

—*Jane*

Knowing I wasn't the ugly duckling I thought I was.

—*Ellen*

Everything was new and exciting and *scary*. Those hormones are irreplaceable!

—*Gayle*

The point of the first boyfriend was to enjoy yourself in romance and see yourself through someone else's eyes. It was about feeling wanted and desired. A crucial follow-up to that enjoyment is finding out what you want and need in a partner, though many of us don't get that far on the first guy.

Those who did said they learned these things from Mr. First Boyfriend:

I'll never forget wearing an old red T-shirt and white denim shorts—my hair a mess—and having him look at me. He thought I was beautiful, and I was utterly amazed that someone would feel that way toward me. It gave me an understanding of the power of love and the realization that the superficial really was just that.

—*Dahlia*

I learned I needed to be with someone who didn't consider himself my intellectual inferior. He needed to be confident of his abilities and feel unintimidated by who I was.

—*Melinda*

It is important for all future boyfriends to have depth, honesty, some sort of brain, a clean reputation, the balls to tell you if he's also dating someone else. Also, never break up with someone on an important day or you ruin it for them. Avoid New Year's, birthdays, and Christmas. Also—the most important thing—I was actually embarrassed later in life to admit to dating him because he was such a "bad" choice.

—*Vera*

Though the pleasure of the experience is fleeting, there's still more (always more) to learn. In dating my Mr. First Boyfriend, I learned some amazing things about myself:

- I can't be pushed around. As crappy as I felt after the breakup (and it was the first time I felt that way, so I didn't know it *wasn't* the end of the world), I never thought of sleeping with Michael to get him back. I knew I wasn't ready yet, and as an adult looking back at the eighteen-year-old me, I'm proud I stood my ground when it would have been so easy to give in to his needs.

- I enjoy the story behind the romance, the psychology behind dating, the often-stumbling dance of two personalities, two sets of strengths and expectations. (Maybe that's why I decided to study psychology at

Penn. Maybe that's why I write the books I do. Who knew these seeds were planted so young. Thanks Mr. First Boyfriend for your part in my career!) Michael stayed on the fringes of my life till I met my next boyfriend. When I started dating someone else, my friend Lisa took great pleasure in telling Michael about my "great" new boyfriend. And—whoosh—Michael was gone. I found it fascinating to see the way he operated: as long as I wanted him, he stayed around but purported to be not the slightest bit tempted by me. When he learned I wasn't emotionally needy anymore, Lisa noted, his face crumpled. The next time I saw him, he had a new girlfriend wrapped around him. (He later dumped her, and she and I became friends. Who needs soap operas when you can create your own?) I've never "just dated" since. I look at who calls whom and who bends a head to kiss first. I keep an eye out for guys who look at dating like Michael did; does he want me or just need me to want him?

○ I now know that Michael influenced the "type" of boy I thought I liked for a long time. I was sure I wanted someone tall and dark and preferably Latin. But when I thought "type," I was thinking only of the surface details. For a long time I didn't consider the important things—humor and wit—or the crucial ones—kindness, maturity, and connection.

And you thought Mr. First Boyfriend was chiefly about learning to kiss.

THE LEGACY OF MR. FIRST BOYFRIEND

In addition to the kissing and the learning about yourself, all the Misters leave a legacy. A piece of each one is carried on to the next romance.

Mr. First Boyfriend's legacy is large and much more important than wanting a certain physical type (I shed this expectation long ago, by the way. So if you're blond, you can still call me). He's setting the stage for the loves and losses to come, so he's got his work cut out for him.

I want to date as though every guy is Mr. First Boyfriend. I want to feel that pride in having him by my side—so he had better be worth it. I want to check in with myself along the way. Is this what I want? Am I being my true self? If it's not and I'm not, I want to know that I can and should let go. I want to remember the feeling of kissing for the first time, the intensity of writing never-sent letters, even the weighted-down, stifling feeling of that damn fluffy bathrobe in the middle of a perfectly beautiful afternoon.

I'm going to date as long as I need to (and my journey's long), and I never want to drag my feet.

And when a guy is wrong, I won't hesitate to move on.

THE IMPORTANCE OF MOVING ON

Healthy women take those bits and pieces of their first boyfriend that worked for them and go on to look for the next guy. Yet New York therapist Jennie Ackerman sees many women who, in contrast to this healthy approach, "use their first significant relationship as a paradigm for future relationships . . . developing unhealthy choices."

A frightening example of this is the girl who grows up in a family atmosphere wracked by violence or drug abuse. In these cases, Ackerman says, by the time the girl develops her first romantic relationship, she is already "conditioned" to accept what is unacceptable to a healthier girl. She often derives satisfaction from a relationship that brings chaos with it. Her Mr. First Boyfriend may be verbally or physically abusive, drink too much, or cheat, and because she never mastered whatever problem existed in her family, she stays with the relationship as she unconsciously attempts to "get it right" this time.

In Billie's case, she's not sure why she got into an abusive relationship, but she made sure it was her last (and in doing so, she made her own legacy):

We went to high school together. He was actually the goofy kid who lived around the corner, the tallest kid in school, who wore the Coke-bottle glasses. His personality wasn't that of the typical nerd, but he sure looked like one upon first meeting. I was always taught to believe that I didn't need a man in my life, that nobody should treat me badly. Everybody who ever met me would describe me as confident but quiet. In this relationship, however, I somehow couldn't defend myself. I just put up with his controlling behavior. I learned from my experience how women in abusive relationships can stay. Here I was, someone who from the outside used to think how could any woman ever let a man do that to her? yet when it was happening to me it was a very different situation. Now I don't put up with controlling behavior at all. Being with him has also made me fearful, though, of ending up in another controlling relationship. This leads to my tendency to end relationships before they ever get going. It's also unnerving how some things people say always stay with you. I remember him telling me, "Don't you ever get fat."

When you find yourself repeating unhealthy Misters or you have difficulty letting go of their hold as you start future relationships, therapy can be a big help.

Sometimes, after we try out romance, we move on to Mr. First Love. Sometimes Mr. First Love is also Mr. First Boyfriend. More commonly though, as we'll see in the next chapter, he's the guy Mr. First Boyfriend prepared us to enjoy.

Been There, Learned This

- Before there can be a last boyfriend, there's got to be a first. Good, bad, or ugly, Mr. First Boyfriend is the jumping off point for our romantic life.

- Every guy is a potential Mr. First Boyfriend. There's no room for the jaded in dating. Rather than simply the first chronologically, he may be the first boyfriend you let read your fiction or he may be the first boyfriend you travel through Asia with. However you do it, seek that freshness, that intensity.

- Mr. First Boyfriend can teach us that we need to look beyond the "type." Sure, personally I love 'em tall and dark, but smart and kind has taken me further.

A THERAPIST WEIGHS IN

Most girls choose their first boyfriend for shallow and physical reasons. The primary draw is the physical and the secondary is his status (Is he the star football player? Does he have a car?). Some of us replicate family issues, and only stop when we become conscious of what we're doing. Most of us change what we're looking for in our twenties. Some change in their thirties, and some women in their forties stay stuck with the shallow and choose the same criteria in first and last boyfriends.
—Lisa Slade-Martin, Ph.D.
Washington, D.C.

Check Yourself Quiz
DO YOU TREAT HIM LIKE MR. FIRST BOYFRIEND?

Answer "Yes" or "No" to each question. Then use the scoring section to check whether he's Mr. First Boyfriend.

_____ 1. I get a jolt when I run into him, but he'll never know.

_____ 2. I like to bring his name up in conversations. Often. Preferably proceeded by "my boyfriend."

_____ 3. We talk for hours on the phone.

_____ 4. The thrill of our relationship is trying hard not to get caught in various states of undress.

_____ 5. I regularly blow off my female friends to see him.

_____ 6. I can picture marrying him one day—and I've told him.

_____ 7. Our relationship involves doing things—fast, illegal, or just fattening—that I'd never have the guts to do alone.

_____ 8. He's better for me in my mind than in person.

_____ 9. We regularly lose track of time when we're kissing.

_____ 10. I'll remember him, always.

SCORING

1.	Yes: 0	No: 1	6.	Yes: 0	No: 1
2.	Yes: 1	No: 0	7.	Yes: 0	No: 1
3.	Yes: 1	No: 0	8.	Yes: 1	No: 0
4.	Yes: 0	No: 1	9.	Yes: 1	No: 0
5.	Yes: 1	No: 0	10.	Yes: 1	No: 0

0–5   Sounds more like a different Mister—Puppy Love, Dangerous, or even First Love.

6–7   He could be the first boyfriend.

8–10   Yep, you're displaying all the signs. Say it loud and proud: He's my _boyfriend_.

SURVIVING MR. FIRST BOYFRIEND

You knew it was a roller-coaster, but did you realize that getting through your first relationship was an accomplishment? Sociologists Kara Joyner and J. Richard Udry looked for connections between teenagers' romantic status and psychological status, and they found that those in love were slightly more likely to be depressed. The rates of depression were higher for girls than boys. Reasons why the thrill of the first boyfriend might nonetheless hurt like hell included the fights teen girls have with their parents over dating and the possibility that love for young women goes hand-in-hand with a dip in self-esteem, as they fret over impressing and keeping their loved one.

Love may be grand, but it's been proven that the first experience is also pretty rough. Here's to adulthood!

Cornell University News Service. "Puppy Love's Dark Side: First Study of Love-Sick Teens Reveals Higher Risk of Depression, Alcohol Use and Delinquency." [www.news.cornell.edu/releases/May01/teenlove.ssl. html], May 21, 2001.

MR. FIRST BOYFRIEND: JUSTIN TIMBERLAKE

Britney Spears locked eyes with *NSYNC's Justin Timberlake back on the *Mickey Mouse Club* set. But it wasn't until the two doffed their mouse ears and grew up (a little) that they really noticed each other. Justin was Britney's first boyfriend. Then someone cheated on someone, Justin released his first solo album with the bitter anti-Britney cover song "Cry Me a River," Britney dropped out of showbiz for a year's vacation, and Justin danced on tabletops with Cameron Diaz. Could you take the drama?

PROS
- He might serenade you, with all the latest dance moves.
- You could get a song written about you.
- You probably could ride free at Disney World.

CONS
- Can you say "momma's boy"? Could you handle her knowing *all* the details of your relationship?
- He keeps saying he'll always love Britney. Move on, boy.
- He left Britney, he left *NSYNC. Doesn't seem too loyal.

Chapter 5

Mr. First Love

Our first love is when it all comes together. We move forward from the frisson of excitement at seeing someone (but never touching him) and from the delicious bragging rights of calling some guy "my boyfriend" to the relationship in which we actually fall in love. Sure, I'm biased, but I see young women who fall hard for their high school sweethearts, who fall hard back, and the next thing you know they're schlepping the kids to Disney World, and I think, "Where's the fun in that?"

My tenth-grade English teacher, Tek Young Lin, told his students that good cannot exist without evil. This idea seemed unfair at the time, but he was sure of it, and he showed us the balance by angling two students up against each other, back to back, and explaining that if evil were to disappear, then good would topple. Lin's point was this: if we had no evil, how would we recognize good? And in the case of love, without the journey, how exactly do you recognize the destination?

Would pulling the sword from the stone have been that big a deal if it weren't wedged in so deep? The joy of the journey to find your first love is so delicious and hard-won, like a cup of perfectly bitter hot cocoa with a mound of sweet whipped cream on top. I'm sorry for anyone who actually married her high school sweetheart and never tasted the too cold, too sweet, too small libations first.

I mooned over Sammy and had the bragging rights with Michael. Then I met Matt and I fell in love. I stepped off the elevator in my Penn dorm and turned to walk down the hall to my apartment. "Excuse me," came a voice from behind. I turned to face the voice, and its owner—completely unselfconscious in the way of fraternity members on a dare or hazing mission—said, "My fraternity is having a formal and my friend needs a date. Would you come?" And I, flattered and naïve, said, "Sure." My date, a skinny, smiley kid, packed a condom in his wallet for the dance but was completely respectful. I met his friends around a table and ate and danced with them till early in the morning. We all took a cab home, and when they dropped me off, I leaned into my skinny, smiley date and gave him a light kiss and a thank-you. His friend, Matt, who had gone to the dance with his on-again, off-again high school girlfriend, was the one to call me. He told me how impressed he was that I had taken the dance seriously and kissed my date out of politeness. He told me about the contents of his friend's wallet and how I had made his night, regardless. He asked me to the movies and I sat side-by-barely-touching-side with him throughout *Pumpkinhead* (a ridiculous slasher film whose protagonist had the unfortunate inability to remove a large squash from atop his shoulders), thinking of him next to me. It was a giddy feeling I hadn't encountered the entire evening at the dance, and when Matt kissed me at the end of a long walk through campus a few nights later, up against a chain-link fence, grenades burst inside me.

LOVE IS A MANY-SPLENDORED THING

When I was small, I asked my mother why so many of the songs on the radio were about love. "It's what makes people want to sing," she told me. And that's how it felt with Matt. To be with him, talking earnestly about life and our place in it, to kiss and figure out what felt good, to want so much to listen to his ideas and hopes, made me burst into song (and dance) back in my dorm. It was heady and grounding at the same time. I don't think I'd ever been taken as seriously as Matt took me. I was nineteen and scattered; unhappy at an Ivy League school where everyone seemed more interested in drinking and eventually making as much money as Donald Trump, the mascot of the dominant business school, than in changing the world. My parents urged me to keep my eyes on the goal of graduation, but I longed to drop out. One winter Saturday I volunteered at a local soup kitchen. The difference between the dignity of the bone-tired homeless men who bled into the room for their one meal of the day and the hazy, mortally bored stance of the privileged kids I studied with struck me deeply. I went home that night and told Matt about the men. How one man said to another, "Christmas is coming soon," and the first man, bowed over his full plate said, "Any day with dinner is Christmas." Matt wrote it on a piece of paper and taped it to his wall, and I was inexplicably grateful to him for caring.

I felt understood and desired. And my world changed. It was remarkable. I had thought that getting out of Philadelphia was the only way to be happy again. Now I was suddenly joyful right where I was. Though the best-case scenario would have been dropping out with Matt and cruising the country in a beat-up convertible, we were far from that footloose. (We were in fact so cautious that we didn't dye our hair matching shades of blue-black one night—the appeal was strong—because we were going on interviews.) My parents couldn't possibly know the dividends their checks to the university were paying. I was learning so much: how to think about someone else's needs and enjoy the deep sense of satisfaction that comes from meeting their challenges; how to express what I needed and yet compromise to make our differing needs fit together; how to leave a frat house in the morning without being seen by the other guys.

THE HARDER THEY FALL

Of course the cynics among us will say, the harder you feel, the harder you fall. And unless you stay with your first love for the rest of your life, the end has got to come at some point. Matt and I broke up and reconnected over and over throughout college until our senior year, when he taped a rose to my door and said we needed to talk. He had decided we should marry. He'd convert; he'd ask for my father's permission; we could even move to Israel if I wanted (I had returned from a semester abroad in love with that country). And I did the worst thing possible in the mind of intense Matt: I laughed him off. Marriage? We were twenty-one. Marriage? As in forever, growing old, having kids, owning something? He left in a huff for the final time.

But many women end up heartbroken the first time they give their heart away. Several recounted to me the agony of that breakup:

He said he was breaking up with me because I wouldn't sleep with him. I thought I was too young and not ready to make that decision. He said our relationship wasn't really "going" anywhere. I didn't see why it had to go anywhere. I was so happy about where it was.
—Vera

He was my high school sweetheart and I was queen of his world; whatever I wanted, I only needed to ask. But we both desperately needed to grow up. And because we were with each other for so long, we were afraid to change, for fear of the fact that the other would not accept it. There was so much drama in being together and so much pain in breaking up. It felt like the end of the world.
—Hope

I flew up to meet him for a week, which rapidly went from great to disastrous. The exact moment I knew it was over was when we were at the movies and I put my hand on his leg. He didn't flinch, didn't look at me, didn't move toward me, didn't do anything. I sat like that for about thirty seconds, removed my hand, and tuned out the rest of the movie. We didn't speak a word the rest of the drive back to his parents' house. There were two days left before I went home, and I knew I had to get my feelings out. I tore out a blank page from a book I found downstairs, and I wrote out every last heart-wrenching word I could think of to express my feelings. We drove to the airport a day later, and I gave it to him. He gave me a picture of him with "Sorry it didn't work out" scribbled on the back and that was that. I got on the plane bawling. The poor old man who sat next to me probably thought I was having a breakdown.

—*Natalie*

BREAKING UP ISN'T THE BOOBY PRIZE

This is where I gather the weary, the bitter, and the fed up. As they nurse their wounds and grimace, I can see them all before me, wondering why in the hell I had to dredge up such painful memories. They've forgotten the naïve, trusting girls they were, and it's better that way. They don't want to remember what it felt like to love so completely that when it ends they feel like Wile E. Coyote when he steps off a cliff and falls only after looking down and realizing that his solid ground has disappeared.

I have two choices here: I can wax philosophic—offer these weary, pained women jasmine tea and a soft pillow with a furry cat wrapped around it while I talk in low, soothing tones. Or I can do what needs to be done: tell 'em to get over themselves.

It's just like good and evil, back to back so they won't topple: to fall deeply in love you've got to work your stiff self into that accommodating deep squat so that vulnerability can balance alongside you. To fall in love, you've got to accept the probability of breaking up.

I don't believe in "poor me," and I don't believe in wrong choices. I can match your psychic scars slash by slash. Want a portrait in pain? Take a look at photographs of me a month after my fiancé called off our wedding—I'm so painfully thin my collarbones jut forward far enough to collect rainwater. So what?

Our belief that there are always victors and victims is exactly the fertile earth needed to make getting married appear to be a mark of success. He loves you! You love him! You win! Maybe you found him early and never had to experience the pain of breaking up. Or maybe you overcame adversity (saying goodbye to Misters who—horrors!—didn't want to stay forever) and landed the prize.

Getting married isn't the Holy Grail, and breaking up isn't the booby prize. Mr. First Love matters just as much ten or twenty years later as he did back then. In time we do get over the pain, and what we're left with is the memory of the best times—of Matt and me in our tortured youth, a certain time of life that could never (thank God) be recreated. I just did a Google search for Matt and found that he's an English professor at a college in the Midwest. One Web site carried pictures of him guest lecturing on his first book. His smile and dimples are the same. Different is the gold band on his left hand. Crazily nostalgic as I tend to be, I wanted to e-mail him and thank him for the memories that are welling up in me. I thought better of it. It's enough to remember him from a distance. The memories are precious, and as with the remembrances of other Misters, I'm so very happy to have them.

Our next Mister is never a memory: he's with you for good. He's Mr. Best Friend.

Been There, Learned This

○ Connecting deeply with someone else opens up the world.

○ Loving someone else is worth it, even if you get your heart broken in the process.

○ You can live through heartbreak, and yep, it's better to have danced than to have just sat against the wall.

○ Stop whining about old pain, and channel it to move on to better and better experiences.

A THERAPIST WEIGHS IN

Very often, our choice of a first love shows we're trying to get needs met that have not been met before or, the opposite, following a pattern we're comfortable with. People very often repeat patterns of communication they saw in their own family. This can have a profound effect on future relationships.
—Miriam Stern, LCSW
Cherry Hill, New Jersey

Check Yourself Quiz
WHAT'S THE IMPORTANCE OF
MR. FIRST LOVE TO YOU?

Answer "Yes" or "No" to each question. Then use the scoring section to check whether you understand the importance of Mr. First Love.

_____ 1. I've completely forgotten his name.

_____ 2. Nobody has measured up to him since.

_____ 3. It hurts too much to think about him.

_____ 4. We didn't last, but the memories do.

_____ 5. I learned how to kiss—enough said.

_____ 6. I'd like to go back and tell him I'm sorry.

_____ 7. I worry that I'll keep picking guys like him.

_____ 8. He was a jerk, and I'd rather not talk about him.

_____ 9. I still have love letters from him in a box in the closet.

_____ 10. I still have his number on speed dial. Just in case.

SCORING

1.	Yes: 0	No: 1		6.	Yes: 0	No: 1
2.	Yes: 0	No: 1		7.	Yes: 0	No: 1
3.	Yes: 0	No: 1		8.	Yes: 0	No: 1
4.	Yes: 1	No: 0		9.	Yes: 1	No: 0
5.	Yes: 1	No: 0		10.	Yes: 0	No: 1

0–5   It's important to put him in his place: in your closet or in the back of your head. He was just one of the many guys to come.

6–7   You're halfway there. Give him a little less power over your future.

8–10   You know the importance of Mr. First Love: a good, faded memory and a jumping-off point.

YOUR FIRST LOVE STAYS WITH YOU

How you remember your first love can heavily affect your ability to bond in the future. That's the hypothesis of University of California-Berkeley graduate student Jennifer Beer. She collected the first-love stories of 303 Berkeley undergraduates and identified four patterns of perception surrounding relationships:

○ Secure: a positive sense of both self and partner in a relationship.

○ Dismissive: a positive sense of self but not of partner.

○ Preoccupied: a positive sense of partner but not of self.

○ Fearful: negative recollections of both.

Beer found that those with better memories of their first loves were more likely to view both themselves and subsequent partners more positively. This outcome makes sense—if you fall for a first love who turns out to be a total creep, it's going to be harder to trust yourself the next time around. And the next.

So remember the good in Mr. First Love—and more important, be kind in your memories of yourself from that time. It'll help you better enjoy the Misters to come.

Scalise, K. "After the Breakup, Your 'First Love' Never Really Leaves You, According to Student Research at UC Berkeley." UC Berkeley media release. [www.berkeley.edu/news/media/releases/2001/02/07_love.html], Feb. 7, 2001.

MR. FIRST LOVE: PRINCE CHARLES

Diana was nineteen and shy when the prince galloped into her life and heart. He asked her to marry him with an eighteen-carat sapphire, and millions around the world watched them wed. And where did virginal first love get her? We say we want a prince to call our own, but would you date Charles?

PROS

° You'll live in a real castle.

° You'll have opportunities to give that stiff royal wave.

° You'll get attention for your favorite charities.

CONS

° He's a momma's boy.

° He's never held a real job.

° He's unable to show emotion.

Chapter

6

Mr. Best Friend

HARRY: ... [N]o man can be friends with a woman that he finds attractive. He always wants to have sex with her.

SALLY: So, you're saying that a man can be friends with a woman he finds unattractive?

HARRY: No. You pretty much want to nail 'em too.

—*When Harry Met Sally,* 1989

Men nod at this now-classic sentiment, but women shake their heads. Sure, a man might want something more, but if a woman makes it clear that she doesn't and sets him straight, a purely platonic friendship *is* possible.

You might not think to put best friends in the category of Misters, but if you don't, you are missing out on some interesting life lessons. The fact is that men can be important friends, and a close relationship without sex and romance can be a fun and valuable experience.

"You know him," Eloise said of her Mr. Best Friend:

> The trusty, dependable, always there when you need him guy. Always listened, just a great person. We were a lot alike and knew a lot about each other. I just never felt that click—when he held my hand and there was nothing, that's when I realized it, and it was actually sad because he would make a great boyfriend.

THEY'RE ALL AROUND YOU

Mr. Best Friend usually falls into one of five categories:

Mr. Gay Friend

Eloise dated a lovely guy who always put her needs first. "I love orange Starbursts, and he would always give me all of his orange ones," she remembers. Then she wised up—his kindness was simply that and his romantic attention tended to focus . . . elsewhere. Her Mr. Best Friend was part of a special subsection of best friends. To paraphrase Jerry Seinfeld, if he's single in his thirties, thin, and neat, the chances of getting him to play for your team are pretty slim. I hate clichés and stereotypes, but in the world of sitcoms, he's gay. (Not that there's anything wrong with that.) Eloise dated her Mr. Gay Best Friend before realizing it wasn't going to work, but many of us know the score from the beginning and revel in a friendship that offers the best of male attention, without the sex.

> Robert's my best friend. We talk about everything, ogle the same men. I could say he's just like my favorite girlfriend—we shop and giggle—but that wouldn't be fair. He's a guy, and when he hugs me or tells me I look great, I love it because it's attention from my favorite guy. Who happens to be gay.
> —Lori

He's valuable all right—a fount of insight into men and shared passion, both serious and silly—all without the sexual tension.

Mr. Meant to Be Best Friend

And of course the guy doesn't have to be gay for your relationship to be strictly a friendship. (Why is this so hard to understand? Why did people ask me if my fiancé was gay when we broke up, as if that could be the only explanation for breaking it off with someone two weeks before the Big Day? For those eager to cast aspersions, no, he's not.) The world is full of Mr. Meant to Be Best Friends—guys at work, guys in your local softball league, and all those guys you've known since elementary school.

My happiness would suffer if I didn't have Larry (eighteen years of friendship), Tino (seventeen years), and Brog (nine years) to talk to. It's not me and it's definitely not them—I couldn't possibly remember all the girlfriends Tino, Larry, and Brog have had over the years—it's us together.

Take Tino, for instance: he's always regaling me with

stories of his freaky ability to attract women. He was recently at a concert and a woman standing near him accidentally brushed him with her cigarette. She leaned in to apologize above the din. Tino said when her cheek brushed his, he had to kiss her. So he did. Wordlessly. Just leaned in and they kissed for what felt like hours. She's coming into town to see him next week. Years earlier, another woman, a long-time girlfriend, ran out after him when he broke up with her. She tore down the steps of her building and, as he looked on in horror, dropped to her knees in the street and started banging her head on the pavement. Every woman he has ever dated has phoned him, sometimes years down the line, to ask if he'd consider having another go at a relationship. And yet Tino and I have marveled that if we were the last two people left on earth, humans would die out. Not even the threat of extinction could get us into bed together. We produce no sparks, just friendship. Larry, Tino, and Brog are my extended family. It's a comfy place to be, and one that Sally understood but Harry couldn't wrap his mind around.

Mr. Can We Just Be Friends?

Sometimes a guy falls for you, and it just isn't reciprocal. But does that mean you have to end the whole relationship? Not necessarily. In some if not all cases it's possible for him to settle for being Mr. Best Friend, at least for a while.

Mr. Best Friend can impart a valuable lesson—not every encounter with a Mister has to be romantic, and not every guy who falls for you has to be kissed. Sometimes a frog is going to stay a frog.

I learned that even though someone has all the qualities you are looking for, he may not be right for you, that you cannot force passion. If it is not there, then it is not there.

—*Beth*

We could talk about everything. He could tell me the guy's-eye view. There was nothing not to like about him; he'll make someone a great husband. But we kissed once, and I started laughing and said, "If I had a brother, this is what kissing him would be like." He was disappointed but he was happy I was honest! We're still friends ten years later.

—*Sarah*

It's the flip side of the fairy tale of romance: he's tall, dark, and handsome, listens to everything I say, and kisses like . . . my brother. Did you just hear that bubble burst? It's the entrance of Mister Can We Just Be Friends?—the guy you're crazy about but just can't muster romantic feelings for.

Ah, but we've been in this guy's shoes too, haven't we? We've all had the friend we wish would get a clue and notice us. I have one of those. Doesn't he see that we're so good together? I've known him forever and not one of his girlfriends was good enough. Doesn't he realize the rarity of what we have—the laughter, the camaraderie? I imagine I already know the truth: he does see what I see, and he's perfectly happy keeping us platonic. (His girlfriends have all been much more stylish than I ever could be, by the way. If owning Jimmy Choos or Manolo Blahniks is a nonnegotiable part of a relationship for him, then, yes, we're better as friends!)

There's nothing crueler than that one-sided sexual attraction when you're the one breathing heavy and he's sitting there at the other side of the table clueless (or at least politely pretending to be clueless), and instead of saying the words you've been longing to hear about how he feels it too and what the hell has taken the two of you crazy kids so long to speak up, he says, "Hey, Rache, pass the salt."

I've weighed the two sides here, alone and with friends: the option of outing myself and declaring my feelings ("Well, speaking of salt and other spices of life . . .") and the terrible, friendship-altering silence that would most likely follow versus keeping my mouth shut and enjoying our friendship as I always have, platonically. And I've always chosen the latter. "Here's the salt," I say, and whip it down the table to him. Cutely. Of course I've also been the one who asks for the salt at those critical moments, and I think both parties know the score. No reason to upset a great friendship over it. I've never seen a woman, or a man for that matter, able to rationalize someone else into feeling sexual chemistry.

Mr. to Hell with Sexual Tension

And even when you both do feel that chemistry, sometimes it just isn't fated to be. Remember that Howard Jones song "No One Is to Blame"? I used to think that was the saddest song on the planet. Why couldn't they just make their attraction work? Now, older than thirteen and, I hope, wiser, I've seen quite a few situations where it's necessary to walk away. Sometimes, he just has to be Mr. to Hell with Sexual Tension, Let's Stay Friends, even when it feels like hell.

I love my best friend's husband. Really love him. We seriously finish each other's sentences sometimes. If they weren't together, I'd be all over him.

—*Jackie*

But they are together, and you love your friend, and there is no such thing as Mr. Adultery (or there shouldn't be). Or he lives abroad and he visits every six months. The tension is delicious, the banter makes you feel witty, but the rewards are just not worth the torment of a long-distance relationship, and you're not interested in having him be a Mr. Sex.

Not that it's easy to be friends with Mr. to Hell with Sexual Tension. It takes willpower, maturity, and plain good sense to not run, to stay friends, and to keep it that way. Good for you!

Mr. Family

It goes without saying that sexual tension isn't going to be a problem here (and if it is, you need a different kind of book from the one in your hands). My brother always talks to me straight and can also crack me up like no one I know. And with tutoring from his very sweet wife, he's become very complimentary. And then there are my cousins. As a little girl with big crushes on my older cousins I secretly hoped you could marry extended family. And as an adult I got a call from a cousin when my fiancé and I split, to assure me that the best way to get over my grief was a solo trip to Vegas. I was staying with a friend, bunking on her spare futon at the time, and hearing his voice, steady and sure, helped me sleep that night. Male family can be very important friends in your life, not to be overlooked or unappreciated.

PLATONIC POWER

Gay, straight, or family, Mr. Best Friend helps us remember that it's not all about sex. It seems a simple lesson, but in our overtly sexual society, where it looks like every eleven-year-old feels the need to expose her belly with low-rider jeans, choosing to have nonsexual relationships with men is a message of empowerment. Life—and its Misters—is a smorgasbord, and I'm all for eating your way through rather than rushing to settle down with the plate you are already holding. But my message shouldn't be confused with a battle cry to bed hop.

I'm a big fan of writer Dalma Heyn, and there's one of her messages I'd like to plaster on billboards across the country: "As women, our sense of self is integrally bound up in our relationships; we feel a moral imperative to make and maintain them; this is our job, and our self-esteem is linked even today to how well we do it. Our fears, all available studies suggest, revolve around one and only one theme, the threat of loss."[1]

It is precisely here that Mr. Best Friend is so important—our lives can, and should, be about more than sexual triumph, more than winning over the boy and grabbing the brass (or diamond) ring. If we realize that we have innate worth apart from conquest, we're never going to be threatened by the fear of loss.

I was dating other people, and I kept coming to him to talk about things I normally would have talked to my girlfriends about. I think the main reason I didn't think he was the one for me was because we had started out as friends and I didn't want to blur the boundaries of friend and boyfriend. But also he has an incredible nurturing side to him, almost to a fault. It's almost like he needs someone to take care of all the time. When he told me he wanted to be more than friends . . . I had to tell him I didn't see us that way. I was so afraid of hurting him that I was crying when I was explaining this to him. . . . The thing I realized was you don't have to date every guy who comes around. And he really wasn't the kind of guy I needed.

—*Natalie*

How's that for self-knowledge? The Misters are about getting to know yourself better, however the relationship plays out.

I've never liked the statement "just friends," as if a friendship with a guy isn't a worthy investment. All the Misters are worthwhile, and most for reasons you'd never even think of. This is true even for Mr. Younger—whom we visit next—the man you'd happily rob the cradle for.

Been There, Learned This

- Friends are invaluable. They don't need to be anything more than that.

- A little sexual tension never hurt anybody—even if only one of you is feeling it.

- It's natural for us to love men, and not just for romance.

- It's valuable to hear the male point of view and enjoy male companionship free of a sexual agenda.

A THERAPIST WEIGHS IN

I've heard repeatedly that woman talk to male friends and brothers and have gotten a window into how men think and how they perceive other women. For that alone, male friendships are invaluable. In addition, the wider your circle, the more experience.
—Jennie Ackerman, CSWR
New York, New York

Check Yourself Quiz
DO YOU NEED A MR. BEST FRIEND?

Answer "Yes" or "No" to each question. Then use the scoring section to check whether Mr. Best Friend is for you.

_____ 1. Do you have to feel sexually irresistible to every man?

_____ 2. Can you count the number of male friends you've ever had without using all the fingers on even one hand?

_____ 3. When a guy starts to talk to you, do you assume he's interested in more than a friendship?

_____ 4. Do you have a brother or male cousin you love?

_____ 5. Do you have a trusty guy friend to help you understand the minds of men?

_____ 6. Have you ever felt the pleasure of ogling men with a gay friend?

_____ 7. Do you think Harry was right when he said that men and women can't be just friends?

_____ 8. Have you ever dated someone and tried to force yourself to feel a spark?

_____ 9. Do you think "platonic guy" is an oxymoron?

_____ 10. Do you love men?

SCORING

1.	Yes: 1	No: 1		6.	Yes: 1	No: 1
2.	Yes: 1	No: 1		7.	Yes: 1	No: 1
3.	Yes: 1	No: 1		8.	Yes: 1	No: 1
4.	Yes: 1	No: 1		9.	Yes: 1	No: 1
5.	Yes: 1	No: 1		10.	Yes: 1	No: 1

OK, so I stacked this one. I'll let you decide about the other Misters. But if you don't have one, this is an order: get a Mr. Best Friend!

SNIFFING OUT FRIENDS

We look for like-minded people when choosing friends, but who would have thought smell would matter? Carol Ober did. She and her research team at the University of Chicago had women sniffing two-day-old T-shirts and found that women preferred guys who smelled like their fathers. And not just for lovers. They prefer friends to smell like Dad too. This may have to do with our desire to take care of members of our extended family.

Which makes me think: I could spritz every guy I meet with a combination of Ivory soap, Tide, and Gorgonzola cheese and make many more friends.

Pearson, H. "'Eau de Dad' Woos Women: Genes Mean Ladies Like Friends and Partners That Smell Like Their Father." Nature News Service. [www.nature.com/nsu/020114/020114-13.html], Jan. 21, 2002.

MR. BESTEST FRIEND: JERRY SEINFELD

Who said, "The holy passion of Friendship is of so sweet and steady and loyal and enduring a nature that it will last through a whole lifetime, if not asked to lend money"? Sounds like Jerry Seinfeld, but it was actually Mark Twain. Elaine tried a romance with Jerry, but he annoyed her more than he turned her on. The two found that they were much better off as best friends. Think about it: could you date Jerry Seinfeld?

PROS

- He's so damn neat he'd probably take a vacuum to your apartment too.
- He's willing to sit for hours in a coffee shop and talk.
- He stocks every kind of cereal.

CONS

- He has a comment on every little thing.
- He breaks up with women for crazy reasons (man hands, can't remember their names).
- He will never leave New York.

Chapter

7

Mr. Younger

In my freshman year of college a senior and I connected over drinks at the local dive bar. We liked the same books and the same music, and we talked for what felt like hours. My friend Keith drank with us but didn't say much; he just sat with his eyes averted, playing with the condensation droplets that ran down the side of his glass. When the senior got up to fetch more drinks, I beamed at Keith. "Wow," was pretty much all I said. Here I was, all of eighteen, and a twenty-year-old premed student found me interesting, found me smart.

"Oh, please," Keith said. "He'd say anything. He just wants to sleep with you."

I was young and sheltered, and Keith's words just didn't compute. The senior called and took me to see a concert at school. I remember wearing long, intricate earrings, silver-plated and kite-shaped, with an angel etched inside and a fat turquoise bead stuck in the middle. I can remember the earrings in detail, but what the senior said to me to ruin the evening is now lost to time. I remember we were breezily chatting, and then he said something that struck me to my feminist core and turned me right off. And then, seeing my look of horror, he shoehorned in, "Nice earrings!"

Though he called repeatedly and even had a female friend call and leave a message on my voice mail assuring me that he wasn't antiwomen (what on earth *had* he said?), I refused another date. And somehow I also acquired an aversion to older men. There was also the fact that the one time we touched lips proved that the man, however worldly, couldn't kiss.

I tried older men once more. I was living in Israel during my junior year of college. I was twenty and dating a twenty-five-year-old immigrant from Russia. We communicated in a combination of English, Hebrew, and my high school Russian. We were ill suited from the get-go: I was an American with lots of time for travel and hanging out, and he was a poor émigré with a 6 A.M. restaurant shift on top of school. His parents depended on him, his ex-girlfriend back in Russia had hooked up with his best friend, and he was overworked, homesick, and exhausted. He once fell asleep in the middle of a conversation. He just slumped over, and that was that. And one night, after much kissing, he forcefully declared in English, "I am a man. I am not a little boy. Do you understand?" In other words, it became clear, kissing and such was not enough. I wasn't exactly swooning. I ordered him out of bed and got back to my homework.

REJOICE IN HIS YOUTH

It's been Mr. Younger ever since. Back before Demi Moore seduced the sixteen-year-younger Ashton Kutcher and Cameron Diaz began healing the Britney-sick, eight-year-younger Justin Timberlake, I've liked 'em younger. One longtime Mr. Younger, Eli, is eight years and a world younger. I grew up in a traditional home—Mom made dinner and Dad made the bulk of the income. For some reason I've never gotten over the joy at living the flip side of that life. Every time Eli made dinner, I cheered. (I've told all my Misters that nothing turns me on like a man doing dishes. It's not a lie, though it *is* very convenient.)

The appeal of Mr. Younger for me lies in my belief that *no one* has to wear the pants. Eli didn't have the final say just because he was the Mister (who ever came up with that bad idea and made it gospel?). When I made some money writing, I enjoyed taking him out for sushi, smiling to the waitress as I claimed the bill she had laid before him. There's a *Sex and the City* episode in which Carrie earns a fat $25,000 check selling a Japanese translation of her book and buys her boyfriend a beautiful silk Prada shirt. He, whose own book deal has fallen through, balks at the gift. And over time he balks at his beautiful, successful girlfriend. When photographers ask him to step out of the shot so they can take some pictures of Carrie alone on a red-carpet jaunt, he resorts to the most immature breakup ever recorded: good-bye via Post-It note.

Eli watched that episode with me and shook his head: "You can buy me anything you want," he said. Younger guys don't mind a sugar momma. And more important, younger guys cheer on their successful girlfriends.

THE OWW

There's also the pleasure of exerting Older Worldly Woman (OWW) appeal. Just as the senior at Penn won me over just by being older, many young men are attracted to women a few years their senior. And what an ego boost it is to be the more experienced member of a couple:

I was on a long flight to Boston, and we had one of those annoying airline delays that meant we spent hours sitting on the tarmac. A bunch of us were grousing about the wait, and this cute guy directly behind me said something funny, and I laughed. We were both in center seats, so talking was basically a contortionist's project, but we talked—and talked and talked. I offered to switch seats with someone so we could sit next to each other, but no one ever wants a center seat! We talked about him following Phish all over Europe, music, art, history. He was working in Boston for the summer. At the end of the trip, he asked for my phone number, and neither of us had a pen so he ended up with my number written in eyeliner on his ticket jacket.

And he called! And basically invited himself over a week later. He came over at 8 P.M. or so, and at that point I recognized how *young* he was (twenty-two or twenty-three) and I was thirty-three or so. . . . About an hour later he kissed me, and I remember being shocked—*wait*, I'm Mrs. Robinson!!

It made me feel so sexy and worldly.

—*Ella*

Due to my minimum six-day-a-week workload, there really isn't much opportunity to meet people. So I decide to use the Internet as my tool. After peeking at a couple of CompuServe personal listings, I start snooping for matchmaking Web sites. I come across Joe's profile. Cute guy. I'm even more impressed that his answers on his profile are not only complete sentences—they're grammatically and punctuationally correct. *Huge* plus for the boy. As with all dates, we agreed to meet at a central and public location. He chose a multi-club with a piano bar, country bar, and so forth.

I was treated like a queen, and it certainly didn't hurt that he was dressed in jeans and a cowboy hat. An older Michael Jackson song came on, he offered to dance, and midway through I threw my arms around his neck and swayed with him. He laid one on me, and wow! When we were done there, we went to a park. We strolled, talked—and more kissing.

I had known when I contacted him that he was five years younger. My initial thought? "Woohoo! You *go*, girl!"

—*Debbie*

Sometime between whooping "You go, girl!" and letting him go, be sure to stop and remember this: with all the Misters, but especially Mr. Younger, you have a responsibility to the Mizzes who follow. No one enjoys a relationship with a Mister badly bruised from an inconsiderate previous girlfriend. Obviously, you want to treat others as you yourself wish to be treated. It's all the more important with Mr. Younger. Think of the guys you dated when you were young and impressionable. Years pass and their kindnesses and cruelties still resonate. So remember to leave Mr. Younger with a positive view of women. He'll benefit, future Mizzes will benefit, and world peace is suddenly within our reach.

MOMMA'S BOYS

One caveat about dating the young ones: some might confuse a sugar momma with just plain Momma:

I was twenty-five, he was twenty. God, was he good in bed, sang beautiful songs, treated me like a queen. I met him when I moved into an apartment complex and was having a housewarming. A friend and I were setting up, running up and down the stairs getting stuff from the car, when we saw this very cute boy walking an equally adorable dog. So, feigning innocence, I asked him if I could pet the dog. We started talking and I invited him to the party. He never showed up but came by the next day to apologize. He wasn't too smart, but he was so fun.

Since I was unemployed at the time and he was working, I would straighten his apartment, walk the dog, cook dinner, do the grocery shopping. When his mom came to visit, I made sure his apartment was perfect and cooked a great dinner for the three of us. When she turned around and thanked me for taking such good care of her son, I realized that I had turned into his mommy.

—*Greta*

And of course there's younger and then there's just plain young. Beth found that out for herself:

I was home from college and went with a friend to a school event. We were just hanging out and then I saw this cute guy. He seemed to be there by himself, so I figured why not? I talked to him for what must have been four hours that first night. We left the cheesy school event and went dancing, and then my friend and I left for home.

I ran into him a couple of weeks later. Once again we started talking and decided to go get something to eat. That's when I realized he didn't have a car, but I had mine. Keep in mind, not having a car where I grew up is odd because it's so rural you need a car to do anything. I saw him whenever I came into town.

Until I found out through the rumor mill that he was only fourteen. And wasn't even in high school yet.

—*Beth*

If you're looking to stay young yourself, Mrs. Robinson, our next fellow, Mr. Funny, is the man for you.

Been There, Learned This

- Those who call it "robbing the cradle" have never had the fun of the stickup.

- In a world where a woman's value seems to decrease with every new year and new wrinkle, it's a wonderful ego boost to be the Older Worldly Woman.

- It's important to teach your Mr. Younger well so other Mizzes reap the benefits later.

A THERAPIST WEIGHS IN

Dating a younger man can remove the layer of seriousness associated with dating contemporaries. Rather than focusing on "where the relationship is going," involvement with a younger man can mean a focus on living in and enjoying the moment. Time spent together is experienced and enjoyed for what it is rather than what it adds up to or means for the future.
—Sonya Rencevicz, MSW, LCSW
Greenwich, Connecticut

Check Yourself Quiz
CAN YOU HANDLE MR. YOUNGER?

Answer "Yes" or "No" to each question. Then use the scoring section to check whether Mr. Younger is for you.

_____ 1. I can play video games with the best of 'em.

_____ 2. I enjoy sex multiple times a night.

_____ 3. My favorite movie is *The Graduate*.

_____ 4. I prefer a guy with a little salt and pepper in his hair.

_____ 5. I want to be the one who's carded.

_____ 6. I like the idea of being provided for.

_____ 7. I like to be in bed (and asleep) by eleven.

_____ 8. I prefer a guy who remembers the eighties.

_____ 9. I've always wanted to go to the prom again.

_____ 10. I know just the guy, and I think he'd be amenable.

SCORING

1.	Yes: 1	No: 0		6.	Yes: 0	No: 1
2.	Yes: 1	No: 0		7.	Yes: 0	No: 1
3.	Yes: 1	No: 0		8.	Yes: 0	No: 1
4.	Yes: 0	No: 1		9.	Yes: 1	No: 0
5.	Yes: 0	No: 1		10.	Yes: 2	No: 0

0–5   Stick with older guys.

6–7   You could warm up to the bountiful charms of Mr. Younger.

8–11   You know it's true: sometimes men aren't like fine wines.

WILL MR. YOUNGER GO FOR MS. OLDER?

So you like Mr. Younger. What are your chances he'll like Ms. Older? Going by everything we were ever taught in biology class, guys are going to be attracted to young women who appear—thanks to their lush, clear skin and pleasing hip-to-chest ratio—capable of producing lots of little Misters. But a study at Buckinghamshire Chilterns University College, in Britain, finds that's not always true.

You've got a shot with Mr. Younger. But only if you're pretty. Evolutionary psychologist George Fieldman showed men pictures of women, one of whom had previously been ranked by other men as more attractive than the others, assigning the women varying ages in the thirties and the forties and also varying the age assigned to the attractive woman. He then asked which woman each man would choose as a partner. All the men disregarded the ages and chose the beautiful woman.

Maybe, Fieldman surmised, pleasure trumps reproduction. And before you start complaining about that one, think how many times your pleasure urge has won out over *your* reproductive one.

BBC News. "The Lure of the Older Woman."
[news.bbc.co.uk/1/hi/health/1410495.stm] June 21, 2001.

MR. YOUNGEST: ASHTON KUTCHER

He was once just a pretty boy making it on the small screen. Then Demi Moore kissed him, and the little boy became a princely symbol for older women everywhere: we can admire Mr. Younger's buns and have them too. Would you date Ashton Kutcher?

PROS

- He can wear such labels as *boy toy* and *arm candy* with pride.
- He has boundless energy (oh, yeah).
- He plays those cute little pranks.

CONS

- You'll have to get him home before curfew.
- He uses the newest inscrutable hip slang.
- It's difficult getting him into R-rated movies.

Chapter

8

Mr. Funny

If pushed to limit myself to just one Mister, I'd go with Mr. Funny. We look for the familiar, and Mr. Funny is in my blood. While I was growing up, humor and its bedmate, wit, were my family's currency. We'd sit around the table zinging one-liners and building small stories into cantilevered castles in the hopes of making the others laugh. Sometimes the joker managed only to make herself laugh, but that was satisfying too. The best lines and the best stories became family lore, passed down through the generations as others might pass rare gems. My parents cracked each other up for forty years.

When my father fell ill with cancer, the doctor gravely told him, "No matter when you had come in to see me, I couldn't have ever given you more than four months to live."

My father retorted, "I should have waited longer to come see you."

HE MAKES ME LAUGH

When a man makes me laugh, I feel more than a sense of going home. I feel taken care of. Anybody can—and should—make a meal, buy tickets to a show, or listen well. But it takes real caring—not to mention talent—to make your partner laugh.

> My partner makes me laugh and that is one of the things I love most about being with him. His humor is part of his eternal optimism. It balances out my pessimistic tendencies. Many times, if I'm upset or crying, he'll say or do funny things until I stop crying and I'm laughing.
>
> —*Kristen*

> Of course being with someone who is funny is sometimes messy, as it was when he decided to see if he could get a pen to land and stick in a leftover carrot cake.
>
> —*Bailey*

One summer I brought my boyfriend Jason to my cousins' pool for the day. We splashed around, cooled off, and thoroughly enjoyed ourselves. Later, my cousin David told me the Mister floating in the deep end was not the one for me. "He's not funny," he said, in all seriousness. You must understand, this was coming from a man whose father once stood on a long line at the Häagen-Dazs store where I worked as a scooper in high school, and loudly exclaimed, "Your father won't give you money and you have to work *here?* Rachel, come home with me. Take off that apron and just come home." And as I stood there, halfway between mortified and hysterically laughing, he plopped his wallet down on the glass partition and said, "How much do you need?" and started counting bills.

The truth is, David was right. When I tried to put my finger on why Jason just didn't do it for me, it always came back to his premature maturity. Life was serious going for him: Where was he going to live? How could he make more money? We had a Sunday tradition of cranking his stereo way up and dancing daffily around the living room. But one day of mirth didn't quench my thirst for merriment the rest of the week. Life is so hard; I've always felt strongly that my Mister should be an antidote, a place to rest from the outside world. And nothing is better than laughter to make me feel safe, loved, at home.

When a girlfriend marvels, "He makes me laugh," I cheer for her good fortune. Laughter is calming and invigorating— yoga for the spirit. Think of polite office meeting titters or cocktail party half-smile giggles. Now compare them to grab-your-ankles-because-your-stomach-muscles-are-cramped-so-hard laughter. It's duty versus release; civility versus pure joy.

Mr. Funny can take you there.

DID YOU HEAR THE ONE ABOUT . . . ?

If you doubt the importance of a guy who can make you laugh, just think about the alternative: the guy who thinks he's funny but just makes you groan. You know the bloom is off the rose when he doesn't make you laugh. And there is no easier gauge of your compatibility with your Mister than your sense of humor. There's nothing less funny than having to fess up: "Yes, I've heard that story already." "No, I'm not amused by the fact that you can balance a spoon on your nose." Personally I don't see the humor in being mean. I've always shied away from the catty people; as a woman with no fashion sense and sweaters from tenth grade, I find it impossible to laugh at someone else's getup. So a bit on how that suit is *sooo* 1974 will be completely lost on me. And there is no hell fresher than sitting at a table with a blind date who, evidence of my glassy eyes to the contrary, fancies himself a regular Bill Cosby. "Check, please!"

Now, you may ask, What about clowns? Well, there's a reason why I'm not trying to meet men at Ringling Brothers Clown College socials. I don't want my man to be a clown, thank you very much. And there's a reason so many people admit to hating or even fearing clowns. It's that heavy-handedness, that forced mirth, those really big shoes and polka-dotted ties. The clown's ultimate idea of humor—let's see how many of my brethren I can make this Pinto accommodate!—doesn't reflect the real world. The surreal is spooky; it's not funny. (I can fess up now: I dated a professional clown once. When we broke up, my friends delighted in saying, "I'm glad you two broke up. What a clown!" It's not a compliment.)

Because the fact is, when you take the clown out of the big top, he's just a schmo with a red plastic nose.

My sister and I, amusing her husband and ourselves one evening, cooked up a team for *Survivor.* It had the requisite hard-bodies who can subsist on skewered rats . . . and a clown. While the rest of the team was busy building canoes and finding food, the clown was juggling or walking in circles or humming the frenetic big top tune. He was of no use to anybody, and obviously, the first guy kicked off the island. There was no sense to our little riff other than this: What the hell is the point of clowns?

So no clowns or catty remarks, please. But if a Mister can make me laugh—without stabbing anyone in the process, without quoting a movie line (not too original), without balancing silverware on his body, without clowning around, I'm intrigued. Humor done right is intelligence, and intelligence is sexy.

REALLY FUNNY

The real Mr. Funny sees humor in the real world. He spins the everyday into the ridiculous, and have no doubt about it, there's an intelligence in overthinking, as Marianne laughingly appreciates:

> I met Patrick in Costa Rica, where we both taught English at a language school. He had a talent for making everyone laugh, not with slapstick or one-line zingers, but with his ability to see the ridiculous in everything around him. That was a long time ago, but I can still appreciate how he showed me a new, silly way of seeing things.

Once, on a bus trip to the beach, I commented on the palm trees lining the shore. "Look at them," I said. "*That's* where palm trees should live. I feel sorry for the ones in California. They look depressed, living out their lives in some landscaped office park. It's sad, really."

Patrick thought about it for a second, and said, "I don't know, maybe you're looking at this all wrong. Maybe for palm trees, California is the 'big-time.'"

To this day, I'll occasionally stop a moment in front of the gray, worried palm trees that line the supermarket parking lot a few blocks from my house. "Cheer up!" I want to yell. "You've made it!"

Mr. Funny, like Mr. Brainy (discussed in the next chapter), can open up new worlds to you, new ways of seeing, reacting, and enjoying. It's not just the delighted cackle he elicits in the midst of an otherwise hushed lecture hall. It's his ability to tamp down—or scare off completely—the blues and torpor and depression. It's his talent for making the everyday special and funny. He makes our little world bigger, and not by pushing the steel frames of the infrastructure by stuffing clowns into it. As Jean Houston wisely said, between laughing fits, "At the height of laughter, the universe is flung into a kaleidoscope of new possibilities."[1]

Thank you, Mr. Funny.

SHARING A LAUGH

I guess it's my genes, but the ability to make a Mister laugh is about the biggest power trip I can imagine. My ex-fiancé was always saying, "Gee, you're funny," as if he had never realized it before. (Obviously, I couldn't marry him.) He fancied himself a real funnyman, but in truth he wasn't such a riot. Ideally, a couple should spend their time amusing each other, not trying to one-up each other (that's a game for entire families to play).

> My ex once thought he'd be funny about my use of baby oil: "Do you know how many babies they had to squeeze just so you could have that bottle of baby oil?"
>
> My retort? "I'm not too worried about it—they make good use of each baby by grinding up the remainder into baby powder."
>
> I never heard another joke about baby oil ever again. That was one of his flaws—if I deflected something he thought was funny or if I didn't think it was funny, he'd get his BVDs in a bunch.
>
> —*Laura*

My father learned the importance of a couple's laughing together from his father. Way back when my grandmother was a new bride, she won a newspaper write-in contest for the story of how she met my grandfather. Seems they were both invited to the same party, and he asked her to dance. A few minutes into the song, he said to her, "You must be a wonderful cook."

She was, but how could he know? "Why?" she asked.

"Because you can't dance."

Personally, I think I would have been insulted, but his sense of humor and hers clicked, and they were off and running. So many memories of my parents entail the two of them wiping tears of laughter out of their eyes as they amused each other. "See?" my father would say, cocking a thumb at my mother mopping her eyes at the kitchen table. "She's my best audience."

And isn't that who you really want to be with, always? Your best audience. Comedian Victor Borge once said, "Laughter is the shortest distance between two people." Sure, it's great to get naked. But think of the intimacy of private jokes. Laughter's the best medicine, and it makes the day worthwhile. I can't possibly overestimate its powers. Other parents might be able to leave their kids trust funds, but I'm damn happy with my inheritance.

At the end of the day, I want to be with the man who will make me laugh and whom I will make laugh. I'll let you know when I've found him. In the meantime, here's somebody else to think about: Mr. Brainy.

Been There, Learned This

° Laughter is the best medicine, the best entrée, the best way to start and end your day. Mr. Funny epitomizes sexiness, intelligence, and fun.

° It's easy to think of sex when you think of intimacy. But a private joke is just as intimate—and easier to pull off in the subway.

° How his sense of humor matches yours speaks volumes about everything important in a relationship—how the two of you communicate, how (and if) you understand each other, and whether you both find the same things important or ridiculous. It's not enough for others to think he's funny. *You've* got to consider him Mr. Funny.

A THERAPIST WEIGHS IN

Simply, you need someone you can laugh with. If you two can't laugh, it's not good.
—Ruth Greer, Ph.D.
Rye, New York

Check Yourself Quiz
IS MR. FUNNY FOR YOU?

Answer "Yes" or "No" to each question. Then use the scoring section to check whether Mr. Funny is for you.

_____ 1. It's not an apple a day that keeps the doctor away. It's laughter.

_____ 2. Life is very serious business.

_____ 3. I'd rather talk all night, have sex all night, or eat all night. I can get my humor in comedy clubs.

_____ 4. Robin Williams is so funny I don't even notice the hair sprouting off his fingers.

_____ 5. If a man makes me laugh, he's instantly attractive.

_____ 6. A Mister who always jokes is insecure or has a verbal tic.

_____ 7. After a hard day of work, I need a man who'll sit and commiserate with me about how much life stinks.

_____ 8. I own a rubber chicken.

_____ 9. I have incorporated a rubber chicken into sex play.

_____ 10. I know just the guy, and I think he'd be amenable.

SCORING

1.	Yes: 1	No: 0	6.	Yes: 0	No: 1
2.	Yes: 0	No: 1	7.	Yes: 0	No: 1
3.	Yes: 0	No: 1	8.	Yes: 1	No: 0
4.	Yes: 1	No: 0	9.	Yes: 1	No: 0
5.	Yes: 1	No: 0	10.	Yes: 2	No: 0

0–5   You find life a very serious matter and may also find Mr. Funny hard to take.

6–7   You can lighten up! Try Mr. Funny.

8–11   You know the importance of a good belly laugh. Mr. Funny is for you.

THE COUPLE THAT LAUGHS TOGETHER, STAYS TOGETHER

Laughing with your partner doesn't just feel good—it actually strengthens relationships. Cameron Anderson of Northwestern University in Illinois found that over time, couples react more and more similarly to life around them.

Anderson's study, first reported in the *Journal of Personality and Social Psychology*, shows that such "emotional convergence" strengthens relationships and that over time, those more emotionally in tune stayed together whereas more divergent couples split up. It wasn't known whether the couples who displayed increasing emotional convergence over the course of the study had had at least a certain level of similarity back when they first found each other or not. Either way, Anderson says, when you're looking for love, don't discount the importance of laughing at the same jokes and crying at the same movies.

Frisch, D. "Over Time, People 'Catch Mood' of Friends, Lovers." Reuters Health Information. [www.medformation.com/mf/news.nsf /ReutersNews/Over_time_people__catch_mood__of_friends_lovers], May 30, 2003.

MR. FUNNIEST: ROBIN WILLIAMS

What made the sitcom *Mork and Mindy* work was the (who woulda thunk it) underlying tension between beautiful Ivory girl Mindy and her pant-suited alien roommate, Mork. She was cute enough to find actual humans to date and busy enough to not obsess over it. But Mork made her laugh, and she barely kept her attraction to herself. Would you date Robin Williams?

PROS
- He'll give you the gift of constant belly-aching laughter.
- With all that energy, you two are sure to win the all-night dance-off competition.
- You can share clothes with him if you appreciated the timeless style of his Mrs. Doubtfire getup.

CONS
- Every once in a while he tries to be serious and fails miserably.
- He can do a dead-on (and not necessarily flattering) imitation of you.
- He may still own Mork's rainbow suspenders.

Chapter

9

Mr. Brainy

I sometimes wonder if it was the *New York Times* that alerted us to the allure of Mr. Brainy, because I don't know a single girl who doesn't ooh longingly over the idea of couples tucked tight in bed with the Saturday *Times* or sitting across the kitchen table from each other sharing the weekday *Times* or sprawled on the living room floor among moving boxes absorbing the Sunday *Times* (the message being that the Sunday *Times* is more important, and definitely more enjoyable, than unpacking one's new home).

There's something about a man who reads the *New York Times.* He cares about the world! In depth! He appreciates poetry, literature for women, smallish fluffy dogs. He handles his liquor well, and his great thirst for knowledge is never maudlin enough to include memorizing movie dialogue. He's a Renaissance man, a veritable James Bond—without the car crashes or the legions of willing, kittenish lovers.

At least that's my Mr. Brainy. A man smarter than I (smarter than I!) who can teach me something about the world (of course, professional, professorial—even nerdy—Mr. Brainies are welcome too). And believe me, it takes only one relationship with a guy whose conversations are limited to comparisons of the latest action movies to make a girl run straight for the nearest library in search of him.

> I've got a college degree, but I made it through without ever taking a science class. It seemed like he knew everything about chemistry, physics, astronomy. I nodded a lot. I especially liked the astronomy—we'd cuddle under the stars, and he'd tell me all about the constellations.
>
> —*Polly*

> It's not that I couldn't get the material in law school. But his understanding went way beyond that. So to hear him explain the subtle nuances—it was so sexy.
>
> —*Charity*

SEXY AND CHALLENGING

When I asked Gabe, one of my Mr. Brainies, what book he was currently into, he said he was rereading some Dostoevsky. It was only back in his apartment after dinner that I noticed his book was in the original Russian. When a certain congressman made an ill-timed comment on American Jews and the war in Iraq, I asked him why he thought it made such a splash. And his answer took into account so many political facets I never considered that the story seemed to open into new rooms.

There's something undeniably sexy about this Mr. Brainy. You can look at him as he used to be—little Bill Gates in his room building electronics—or you can (and should) appreciate him for who he is today: a giant mind. And even though there's only one Bill Gates, your world is brimming with fascinating Mr. Brainies: the writer who captures exactly what you were thinking; the scientist whose passion for finding a cure for Alzheimer's is matched by the intelligence he applies to making it happen (if anybody finds the cure, it'll be another of my Misters, Alan); the executive who sexily rolls up his crisp white shirtsleeves and explains the stock market. Sometimes the emotional intelligence (EQ) of Mr. Brainy doesn't measure up to his formidable IQ (Gabe was better able to connect emotionally to long-dead Dostoevsky than to the cute girl sitting next to him), but what he has to offer can set your mind ablaze.

And he's more convenient than carrying around a complete set of the *Encyclopedia Britannica.* Confused by the rancor in the Middle East? Momentarily forgotten the name of the ninth president? Mr. Brainy can reference the biblical purchase of land at Hebron and may even breezily mutter, "Harrison. First president to die in office. Pneumonia." Trivial Pursuit, anyone?

There's nothing sexier than a full-to-bursting mind. But intelligence isn't just the ability to consume facts and rattle them off. Intelligence isn't even just about being a brilliant scientist or well-read and versed in all the classics. What Lucy and Patty got from time with Mr. Brainy couldn't have been learned in school:

> He kept me from being intellectually lazy. With him I learned to argue well, think more deeply, and not accept things because "that's the way they should be." I learned how to stand up for myself and defend my own beliefs and ideas in ways I never knew how to do before we started dating.
>
> —*Lucy*

> He wasn't book smart, but he was a thinker. He challenged me. He never let me feel comfortable with the status quo, even if I wanted to be.
>
> —*Patty*

More than being a brainiac, the very best Mr. Brainy gives worthwhile advice, well thought out support, or a passionate, understanding defense of your beliefs. Time with him betters your ability to think logically, to analyze both sides of a standoff, to reason with others, or simply to understand. He might be a Mister with a keen insight into your romance or a deep appreciation of your creative side or a honed sensitivity to the plight of animals. He's the Mister who challenges you to expand your mind.

It's not that you're both math whizzes and you sit around thinking up new theorems. (If you do, good luck to you. Just leave the rest of us out of it.) It's not that you know better than elected officials what would make the most sense in foreign policy. (I've met this Mister and Ms., and I beg of you, don't seat me with them at your next dinner party.) You don't need to have similar talents or hold identical views. Just look at Mary Matalin and her Mr. Brainy, James Carville, to see the sparks between opposite minds. You're welcome to spar with your Mr. Brainy; the only important thing is that he respect you and your intelligence.

What makes a Mr. Brainy is more than scores on tests and breadth of vocabulary. The most important gift Mr. Brainy can give you is the ability to appreciate your own mind. One of my Mr. Brainies is always quick to play devil's advocate. It's not that he likes being contrary. Rather, it's that he enjoys the conversation when our minds are fully unfurled, and not tightly stowed away in our boxes of opinions. He took me to my first 4-H fair. We wandered through the stalls of snorting pigs and prancing goats and majestic, moon-eyed cattle. A pig farmer explained the different types of pigs and talked to us about his life raising animals in Maryland. I asked him earnestly if his kids have any trouble taking ownership of a weeks-old piglet and then, months later, giving it up for slaughter. He turned around and resumed pointing out the different pigs. Mr. Brainy—Harry—and I thanked him and walked on. I started to talk, just a stream of consciousness about how hard it must be to love an animal and watch it go to its death. As we wended our way past the animals, my opinion grew more heated. "Why?" Harry kept asking, after every firm pronouncement. "Why?" He could have offered his own reasonings, but instead, as always, Harry was more interested in watching me work it out for myself.

THE DOWNSIDE

Yet for every Rhodes scholar and deep thinker, there's the Mr. Brainy who gives the smart guys a bad name: he's the guy who *thinks* he's so smart, the Mister with a ridiculous appreciation of his high SAT scores, the one who, maybe without realizing it and maybe downright reveling in it, makes you feel dumb.

> I met him when he was in the midst of completing his master's degree in finance. He was also intellectually compatible with me when it came to most things, but he felt that since he was smart when it came to financial matters, his way was the *only* way when it came to other things too. I realized I need someone smart enough to realize that his way isn't the only way!
>
> —*Mandy*

One Mr. Look-at-Me-I'm-So-Brainy actually told me that trains were an important invention because some people don't like to fly. I think he mistook my amazement that someone could say such a thing for my being impressed into silence. When researching *There Goes the Bride*, I got into a painful debate with a Mister over a study that says that couples who cohabitate before marriage have a higher chance of divorcing than those who wait. I, who had lived with my ex-fiancé and found out how very ill-matched we were—saving us from a torturous and short marriage—see the benefit of living together first. Besides, as I pointed out to this Mister, there's no way to suss out when it's solely the living together that dooms a couple and when it's the fact that people who live together are more liberal and thus more likely to divorce than to stay in a bad marriage. Nope, he told me. The study proves, once and for all, that living together is a bad idea. "After all," he said, "Why buy the cow when you can get the milk for free?"

Huh? "How does that stupid cliché help your argument?" I asked. (Silence.) "How does one study make it all crystal clear?" (Silence.) I threw a million questions his way, but he just sat smiling the Cheshire Cat grin of the self-satisfied. There's brainy, and there's bullying.

So why bother? Ah, you should always bother. There's a theory that we look for people to date who are what we're not and have what we don't. Sometimes it works out that way (as with Mr. Rich, whom I discuss later), but more often the appeal of the Mister has more to do with what we need than with what we're not. Confusing? Read about Mr. Not—the guy you really don't need—to understand it better.

Been There, Learned This

- Talented Mr. Brainies can teach you many important things. Mine have taught me everything from how to build a Web site to how to manage my money. Knowledge is power, and it's damn sexy.

- The passion and smarts of Mr. Brainy can lead you to think outside your own box, to know what's important enough to speak up about.

- Mr. Brainy can lead you to a deeper understanding of the joy of deeper understanding.

○ Even the look-at-me-I'm-so-brainy guy can teach you, however unintentionally, to defend your opinions, to stick up for your beliefs, and to hone your ability to hold your own.

A THERAPIST WEIGHS IN

When dating someone smarter than you, notice: Is he considerate? Does he have the common sense not to speak to you in foreign tongues? Does he relate to you? Differences in intellectual ability can make for a pretty good dynamic—his strengths are here, mine are here—but it's important that he knows who he is and doesn't try to prove he's better than anyone.
—Michael Lunter, LCSW
St. Louis, Missouri

Check Yourself Quiz
ARE YOU IN THE MARKET FOR A MR. BRAINY?

Answer "Yes" or "No" to each question. Then use the scoring section to check whether Mr. Brainy is for you.

_____ 1. If someone corrects my grammar, I cannot be held responsible for my reaction.

_____ 2. I don't understand the point of trying to make a living in the arts. Why not get a real job?

_____ 3. I am not amused by those who endlessly quote movie lines.

_____ 4. I'm threatened by different points of view.

_____ 5. My motto is "Make love now, talk later."

_____ 6. I love a challenge.

_____ 7. If he's wrong on a point, I just smile; I don't want to embarrass him by correcting him.

_____ 8. I'm a slave to a man speaking to me in a foreign language.

_____ 9. I'm impressed by high SAT scores.

_____ 10. I know just the guy, and I think he'd be amenable.

SCORING

1.	Yes: 0	No: 1	6.	Yes: 1	No: 0
2.	Yes: 0	No: 1	7.	Yes: 0	No: 1
3.	Yes: 1	No: 0	8.	Yes: 1	No:0
4.	Yes: 0	No: 1	9.	Yes: 1	No: 0
5.	Yes: 0	No: 1	10.	Yes: 2	No: 0

0–5   Stick to Mr. Dangerous or Mr. Sex.

6–7   You should consider letting a Mr. Brainy into your life. If only to learn a little.

8–11   You've got a Mr. Brainy in your sights. Enjoy!

ONE MISTER EXTRA BRAINY, PLEASE

So what's the best way to make your Mister brainy? Australian researcher Dennis Garlick reviewed 124 studies on intelligence to see how "neural plasticity" stacked up against good old genes. Although smart genes, courtesy of Mom and Dad, better one's chances of growing up an egghead, neural plasticity (the development of neural connections as a result of environmental stimuli) proved even more important. That's because even though those of us with smart parents are better equipped to bend to stimuli, we all needed an active environment to fire us up during our "critical learning period" of twenty years. But if you're worried that your Mister's brain cells are now dying off while he sits inside all weekend watching TV, don't fret. After our critical learning period, we're like old dogs; we don't learn new tricks. In other words, if you drag him away from the television set, he'll be able to act human again. And if he's too heavy or stubborn to drag . . . on to the next Mister!

American Psychological Association. "Is Intelligence Fixed or Enhanced by Environmental Stimulation and Demands? Neural Plasticity Rather Than a General Measure Better Defines the Potentials and Limitations of Intelligence." Press Release. [www.apa.org/releases/iqdebate.html], Jan. 16, 2002.

MR. BRAINIEST: ALBERT EINSTEIN

When *Time* magazine named Albert Einstein Person of the Century, it said that he was "unfathomably profound—the genius among geniuses who discovered, merely by thinking about it, that the universe was not as it seemed."[1] Could you take being around that much brainpower?

PROS
- He would be very handy when you forget what *E* equals.
- If knowledge is power, you've got the arsenal when you're with him.
- Think what other theories the two of you could try to prove.

CONS
- He never brushed his hair.
- What good is profundity if you can't fathom him?
- All those brains don't mean a thing when he's off running around on you. (*Time* also reported that the philandering Einstein said his wife's "pathological jealousy was typical of women of such 'uncommon ugliness.'" Nice.)

Chapter

10

Mr. Not

I opened the door, and there stood Greg. I had invited him to my party a few days before and then promptly forgotten about him. Now he was just outside my door, blond, lanky, and visibly nervous. Hmm, I thought. This could get interesting.

It certainly got interesting, but not only in the ways I had hoped it might. Because Greg was my Mr. Not: so wrong for me, I think of him now and can't keep from shaking my head.

Don't get me wrong: I don't regret our relationship. It's Misters like this that *really* show you who you are and what you want and need. Everyone has at least one Mr. Not—and some of us have many more. Mr. Not isn't every guy you don't marry. He's the living, breathing personification of the roads you're not interested in traveling. He's valuable because having him in your life means you have to step up to the microphone and say, loudly and clearly, "No, not for me, nope." There are reasons the other Misters don't last a life-time (thank goodness). Mister Not is the guy who makes you realize what exactly is wrong for you.

It sounds strange, but it's a powerful feeling. Knowing what you don't want, in guys as in life, puts you closer to fig-uring out what you *do* want. It's even more powerful if you're been involved with Mr. Not for at least a little while (he can very well overlap with the Misters). Maybe you didn't realize his Not-ness at first—or maybe you didn't understand *you* at first. And maybe your priorities changed or you matured or you just got smart.

NOT THE WORLD TO BE IN

Greg, for example, was always unhappy. An attorney at a one-man regional office, he spent his days surrounded by a cloud of papers. He wasn't nervous just around me—he was nervous in his desk-sized office, papers billowing, he was nervous around other people, he was nervous in the comfort of his own home. His skin didn't fit. The only time he felt at peace was when he was praying. He rose early to greet the sun with prayers, and he thanked God throughout the day. Any prayer he could muster, he performed. Any way he could extend it, rocking his body forward, eyes closed, he did.

I don't know if it was God or prayer that gave him solace, but it didn't matter. He took classes on Torah and Talmud once a week but hungered for more. I asked him if he should maybe think about giving up law for rabbinical school. He looked at me, amazed, as if I had just seen deep into his soul. We both knew that rabbinical school meant moving to New York, alone. He wanted to, but something held him back—mainly his nervous, careful character. "Not just yet," he'd say. "Maybe one day." And as he moved slowly toward who he wanted to be, he became more and more my Mr. Not.

We had advanced from dinners and movies to holding hands and calling each other boyfriend and girlfriend and, in the early days, I thought he was going through a stage or was angry with his parents or just distracted. Mr. Not isn't like Mr. Dangerous; it isn't the forbidden about him that draws us in. Instead, we're attracted to the good in him, and then eventually we trip up on the large elephant that's also in the room and that we really can't ignore any longer.

For example, Greg wanted me to spend Shabbat (the Jewish Sabbath) with him. But I wasn't allowed to play music or turn on the lights or even go for my usual run, because it was forbidden by the orthodox religious practice Greg insisted upon. Every meal closed with a long prayer of thanks. We had dinner one night at the home of a religious couple, and the husband never touched his wife. All talk was of God. When we left for the walk home, I turned to Greg and said, "This is not the life I want."

And then, suddenly, I was saying it more and more often. He refused an invitation to attend a concert on a Saturday afternoon. It was a free concert (so he wouldn't have had to carry money on Shabbat), but he claimed it was "not in the spirit of the day." His rationale for not playing the radio on Saturday—it's not right to listen to commercials or suggestive lyrics on a holy day—was unswayed by my suggestion that we listen to a classical music CD. Summer was getting longer, and I refused to wait till eight or nine at night, when the sun went down and Shabbat was over, to go running.

It wasn't that we suffered—we still enjoyed cooking together, talking about politics, hiking in the Shenandoahs, and lazing in bed—but it was clear that in the world outside our time together, we weren't in synch. One late summer day we took a hike through a mosquito-ridden forest. We didn't have enough water, and we had to flap our hands constantly to ward off the bugs. Greg grumbled loudly; I was just happy to be outside. We hiked for hours, but it wasn't until he had dropped me back home, gotten into his car, started it, then gotten out again and rung my buzzer that he could bear to tell me that he was moving to Israel.

His need to live a religious life had grown from a whisper to a scream. He wanted to study Judaism all day, and had signed up with a study abroad program in Jerusalem. I stood in shock. In a week he was gone. I heard that he returned, engaged to a religious woman, after two years of study.

After grieving his loss, I realized I had never wavered in seeking what was right for me. I always spoke up about my needs. And just as important, I cared for Greg in all his complexities. That's the beauty of Mr. Not. He shows you another world—be it in values or in ideas of a good time—and you're not tempted to follow. Though it sounds backward, your saying no, your staying put, helps you grow. Like the other Misters, Mr. Not has real life-changing possibilities. Because he was all wrong, Greg helped me map out what I want and need in a partner and in life.

LOOKING FOR AN OPPOSITE

Once in a while, Mr. Not is a deliberate choice. Beth strode straight for Mr. Not but then woke up—not because he was terrible, but because *she* was:

> After I got out of my relationship with my first love I went looking for the complete opposite. Someone who would really pay attention to me and who was not going to be capable of cheating. Someone I could control, instead of him controlling me. I wanted to tell him where to meet me and when to call me, and then not always be where I'd say I'd be or pick up the phone. Eventually I realized that I was with him for the wrong reasons. I was looking for traits that I normally do not respect or like in a guy. It was totally wrong on my part. I saw that the opposite of what hurt me is not always right for me, that I really should not punish someone else for what another person has done to me.

Usually, though, nobody is the villain (I don't espouse dating those kinds of Misters). Rather, what typically happens is that you and your Mister are getting along and then the edges start to chafe. Hey, you realize, this does *not* work for me:

> I knew pretty early on that our values and personalities wouldn't mesh well for the long term. He was a great guy and I cared about him very much. We were very different though, especially on

religion. We also had very different family structures—he had had a very traditional country upbringing in a "nuclear" home and I had had a more independent liberal upbringing in a "broken" home. We didn't really have conversations that much—he just talked. *A lot.* And he told a lot of the same stories over and over, occasionally at rather inappropriate times.

Except when I wanted to tell him to just shut the hell up because I was tired of listening to him drone on about something, yeah, it felt good to be around him. But I got bored around him many times, and I usually felt guilty about it. He was hurt pretty bad when I left and often asked me if there was anything he could have done or changed about himself that would have convinced me to stay. He didn't have much self-esteem, which is another reason it wouldn't have worked with him. I try to be supportive and encouraging and always try to boost self-esteem, but I just don't have the energy to be a constant crutch for people.

—*Celia*

Like the upcoming Mr. Dangerous and Mr. Rich, Mr. Not helps us see the world through very different eyes. Unlike the other Misters, Mr. Not isn't about coveting a different way of life; he's about realizing the just right-ness of our own:

He was a lot older (seven years my senior). He was incredibly handsome, and I associated older with mature. But he didn't want to settle down . . . ever. He has *major* Peter Pan syndrome. He once said, for example, "So I smoke weed a lot. Is that a problem?" It was a real wakeup call for me. I realized that the values that I have are not necessarily values for everyone.

—*Hope*

Mr. Not is not one of my favorite Misters. But when else can you really see what you're made of? Jane, all of twenty-two when she was dating her Mr. Not, realized her own needs and made a huge effort to be a good person:

> I loved spending time with him, and we definitely had great chemistry. But I always found myself looking at other men. I never told him I loved him, which worried me. Something was always missing. I could never put my finger on it. . . . He had come to spend New Year's Eve with my friends and me, and my roommate asked him in jest, "When are you going to marry her?" because he was giving me "the look" while I was dancing carelessly with my friends. He answered, "Whenever she's ready." When she repeated this story to me a few days later, the look of horror on my face surprised her. I knew I had to end the relationship. He deserved someone who could give him the kind of love that he gave me. Who looked at him like that when he was off laughing with his friends. Who would be as good to him as he always was to me. I cried my eyes out when I broke up with him. It may have been one of the hardest things I've ever had to do.

Mr. Not is about realizing your limitations—and accepting them:

> He was a great dancer, incredibly sexy, kissed great. We met at a dance club. I dated him for a summer while in college. Then again when I moved back to the area after a two-year absence, I saw him at a bar. The first time we dated I loved the way he danced. I thought he was incredibly sexy. He was not drinking when we first dated, but he is an alcoholic. It was sad to watch him fall off the wagon time and again. He smoked pot a lot.

> I wanted to fix him. I learned I had a very strong nurturing side. It
> was agonizing to see him ruin his life with alcohol. I couldn't help
> him. But I learned that I can't fix people. They have to fix them-
> selves.
>
> —*Polly*

Our Misters offer us all sorts of things—adventure, sex, fris-
sons of joy. Mr. Not ultimately offers us ourselves, on a silver
platter. By realizing who we're not, we're declaring who we
are. How can you know that and *not* espouse dating lots of
Misters?

> He was the longest rebound relationship in the history of the uni-
> verse, a good friend who stepped in and picked up the pieces after
> my true love relationship fell apart.
>
> At first he just kept me occupied, then he tried to change me—I
> spent a lot of time not really being me and doubting my life deci-
> sions. He gave me the attention and affection I had been lacking,
> but he was manipulative. Now I know what things are important to
> me in life and won't compromise about them. I had to change or
> compromise my priorities and my "self" too many times with him.
> Now, I stick to my morals and beliefs, and I won't compromise them
> for anyone. I will respect others' decision to be different than I am,
> and I can learn from that, but I have some nonnegotiables that are
> just too important to give up.
>
> —*Vera*

When you've had your fill of Mr. Not, it's time to turn to
a fun Mr. Right Now—Mr. Rich, the man you can consider
over a fancy dinner or box seats at a baseball game.

Been There, Learned This

○ There are reasons to date the "wrong" guy. Maybe you could learn most of them alone, but this way is much more fun.

○ Mr. Not, more than any other Mister, is proof that the concept of Mr. Right makes no sense. Mr. Not's right in some ways (why else would you want to be with him?), but he's also *so* wrong.

○ Mr. Not, in all his not-ness, can show you your own values and how, try as you might, you can't push them aside.

A THERAPIST WEIGHS IN

The relationships in which you learn what you don't want are very valuable. Women go into dating with ideals of what they want. The more experience they attain dating different men, the more they achieve a window into what they *don't* want, which is equally important. But, if the relationship is not remotely positive, why bother?
—Jennie Ackerman, CSWR
New York, New York

Check Yourself Quiz
ARE YOU UP FOR A MR. NOT?

Answer "Yes" or "No" to each question. Then use the scoring section to check whether Mr. Not is for you.

_____ 1. The minute a guy shows himself to be wrong for me, I'm outta there.

_____ 2. I know exactly what I want.

_____ 3. I could see radically overhauling myself to fit with the man I love.

_____ 4. I'm pretty sure of what I'd do in any given dating situation.

_____ 5. If he has values different from mine, I'll show him the right way.

_____ 6. I can date someone whose idea of a good time couldn't be more different from mine.

_____ 7. I appreciate a romance in which we disagree much more than we agree.

_____ 8. With most of my boyfriends, it's a case of he says "potato," I say "potahto."

_____ 9. The men I date are so like me we could be siblings.

_____ 10. I know just the guy, and I think he'd be amenable.

SCORING

1.	Yes: 0	No: 1	6.	Yes: 1	No: 0
2.	Yes: 0	No: 1	7.	Yes: 1	No: 0
3.	Yes: 0	No: 1	8.	Yes: 1	No: 0
4.	Yes: 0	No: 1	9.	Yes: 0	No: 1
5.	Yes: 0	No: 1	10.	Yes: 2	No: 0

0–5   You'd strangle him in a minute. No Mr. Not for you.

6–7   If you'd just chill out a bit, you could enjoy Mr. Not's company.

8–11   Enjoy the pleasure of the wrong guy.

WHY AM I ATTRACTED TO MR. NOT?

It could be because you're on the pill. Tony Little of St. Andrews and Stirling Universities in Scotland surmised that when women aren't ovulating, they're more apt to choose a sex partner based on looks rather than on his ability to care for kids. It seems women who aren't on the pill like men with softer features who (the study stretches to say) are better suited for raising kids. Sounds somewhat suspect when you think of all those women who use alternate forms of birth control and still like insensitive guys. Regardless, Little warns that a woman who stops taking the pill might look over and no longer want the man she's previously been swooning over.

"Does the Pill Change Women's Taste in Men?" *Sex News Daily!* *B*(385). [www.sexnewsdaily.com/issue/b385-012203.html#oral%20 contraceptives], Jan. 22, 2003.

MR. NOT-EST: MICHAEL JACKSON

Lisa Marie, what were you thinking? She is reported as saying that after marrying Michael Jackson she couldn't believe what she had done. But at the time she wasn't above smooching him on camera to prove he wasn't a Mr. Not. Could *you* date Michael Jackson?

PROS
- His funky dance moves may just translate into great moves in bed.
- You like llamas; he's got llamas. Perfect!
- Who wouldn't appreciate Neverland?

CONS
- Scandal sticks to him like a needy girlfriend.
- He hasn't learned that the old saw is "Children should be seen and not heard," not the other way around.
- He's such a big fan of plastic surgery, who knows if you'll recognize him tomorrow?

Chapter

11

Mr. Rich

When women fantasize about their perfect Mr. Right, he's usually rich. Sure, saving the world and inspiring future generations is admirable, but in an ideal world school loans are paid off, the mortgage on the house is manageable, someone else does the heavy lifting, and there's a car or two out front.

When we're being realistic, however, these dreams of affluence turn out to be more flexible. *Newsweek* magazine reports that 50 percent of female college students now completely discount a man's earning potential when thinking about future mates.[1]

I attended college earlier than these women, and we used to call it *ambition*—as in, "He doesn't have to have money but he does have to have ambition"—so he would, we hoped, be rich someday. It wasn't that we all wanted to stay home with our future kids; we just wanted the option. My mother was fast and loose with the "you can love a rich man as easy as a poor man" line, and when I protested that I didn't need much money because all I wanted to do was write, she'd counter with, "Wouldn't it be nice to write in a sunny room all day and not worry about money?" (I've achieved the sunny room part on my own.)

HOW THE OTHER HALF LIVES

So let's consider Mr. Rich. Just like the other Misters, he's not to marry—for now. He's to see how the other half lives, to see how much you enjoy it and crave it or if you find it claustrophobic or shallow. He's for enjoying yourself without constantly calculating how much the evening is going to cost and for getting an insight into your own fantasies and actual needs.

I've had two Mr. Riches. Both showed me a great time, and ultimately they reinforced how little money matters to me.

Ronaldo was attending graduate school while living in Washington with his mother, a representative of the government of a small South American country. I fell for Ronaldo, I can now admit, on the strength of his sublime accent. He was also one of the few Misters I've ever dated who shared my belief that a day spent outside biking, hiking, or running was a perfect day. I didn't fall for Ronaldo's money, but it certainly didn't hurt. He took me to the symphony, to the ballet, and out for great meals. He referred to his father as "the Bank of Dad." Money was paramount to him. He shared that his father had told him and his brothers that if they were not millionaires by thirty, they were failures. When a huge snowstorm buried Washington under a foot of snow, he declared that I shouldn't pay my taxes that year because my street went unplowed. He then admitted, not at all sheepishly, that members of his family never paid their taxes (nobody does where he comes from, he said, by way of explanation). When I took him to dinner one night, he shifted uncomfortably in his seat the whole time. Couldn't he pay the bill? Did I want to split it? His discomfort wasn't about wanting to be generous; it was about who wore the pants. He wore them—he was King of the World, the one to whom others were beholden.

We broke up when he helped a grad school classmate cheat on an exam and couldn't fathom why it bothered me. Apparently having so much money had left him without a moral compass, and he lacked heartfelt ambition and character, always expecting a free ride. I believed that being carefree was one thing; feeling the need to screw the system was quite another (and, yes, by that criterion I should have left him as soon as I heard about the taxes, but did I mention his sexy accent?).

Daniel was also rich—and proud of it even though he liked to play it down. He told me it was a mark of how much he cared for me that he showed me the million-dollar figure in one of his accounts. He bought everything on sale but reveled in his parents' private jet and second home in France. He played it both ways, working in a nonprofit and wearing little woolen vests but driving a monster SUV and owning his own house, all well before age thirty. When he wanted to appear a man of the people (when he was tossing around the idea of someday running for public office, for example), he was the nonprofit, coupon-clipping regular guy in scuffed sneakers. When someone disagreed with him, however, or he felt the world had failed him, he was suddenly entitled to more respect, better service, and top billing, because deep down inside he felt the world owed him quite a bit. Most frightening to me was what he said, out of the blue, when we were talking about our possible future. "What can you bring to the relationship?" he asked, and he wasn't talking about my sense of humor or mean tofu stir-fry.

There are reasons we don't marry all the Misters, but we sure date them. And Mr. Rich can be an awfully fun date.

> He wined and dined me. He knew how to treat a woman right and he taught me to appreciate the finer things in life.
>
> —Alice

> Gifts, gifts, gifts! No one dislikes gifts! I was getting whatever I wanted, as soon as I wanted it. But I realized that money doesn't equal happiness, and I was looking for anyone to fill a void in my life that I was not ready to fill on my own. I am not a shallow person, and I hated how empty it made me feel inside.
>
> —Hope

That's the cool thing about all the Misters. You start dating for one him-based reason, and you find out much, much more—about you. In the case of Daniel, I realized how money—and the purse strings that hold it—can make or break a man. When it came to Ronaldo, I found out, as cheesy as it sounds, that all that glitters isn't gold.

Which is not to say it wasn't fun while it lasted:

> He would travel and leave all his clothes in the hotel where he stayed and tell his mom to buy him new ones, even though he had only worn the others once. His impetuousness and his unpredictability and his true disregard for money fascinated me. His style of life was truly astounding. Being part of it was incredible.
>
> —*Lucy*

> When we first started dating, I didn't even know he had money. But because he did, it made things easier. For the first time I didn't have to worry about having enough money on me to go Dutch or think about what I would do if he didn't have enough money to pay for the tab.
>
> —*Mandy*

BUT WHAT ABOUT YOU?

Mr. Rich can give you a feeling of stability, opportunity, and entitlement you might never have felt before. "I *was* safe; I didn't just *feel* safe," marvels Gayle. But being the thinking woman that you are, you will start wondering, what's the difference between a life of money and your own life? This is where dating the Mister expands outward into figuring out the Ms.

Are you a woman who *needs* the latest fashions? When you hear that long skirts are out, do you shovel up the contents of your closet and give them to Goodwill so you can make room for the micro-minis? Do you keep ditching your current cell phone for ever-smaller versions? Is it fulfilling enough to be an artist, or is it too much of a stressor to watch your hard-earned savings deplete?

Does it puff you up with pride to scrimp and save and have your very own place, or are you always going to toss and turn at night until you've got that million-dollar cushion wedged between you and the welfare office? Perhaps dating Mr. Rich makes you realize that you're a little too susceptible to the fantasy of Mr. Rich riding in astride his white horse and saving the day. Sure, a rich guy might be a nice—even necessary—accessory if it's important to you to not ever have to worry about money. But maybe it's time to realize you're not ever going to be happy as a starving artist or low-on-the-ladder employee and really should go get that MBA.

It's important to suss out when the Misters are fun and good for you and when they just represent something you need to undertake for yourself—like earning your own money or doing some soul searching and therapy to understand your fears.

Some women won't feel safe at all with a Mr. Rich and find that money in excess leaves them off-kilter. What it takes to buy their peace of mind is less about dollar bills and more about family, a strong system of friends, and solid-enough shoes and a super supportive bra for long runs. No Mister can ever be everything to you. And all the Misters put together aren't the whole puzzle either.

Some women build unreal expectations about Mr. Rich that are crushed by the kind of self-centered narcissism that often comes with a fat bank account:

He had all this money, but the kicker was that he actually didn't spend it on me! One night around my birthday he had to work so he came by later. He had a handful of flowers when I answered the door—there were about seven or eight different ones. I told him thank you, and he said, "I would have gotten you more but they were stepped on." I looked at him quizzically and said, "Stepped on?" And he said, "Yeah, you know when the audience throws flowers to the people on stage after a performance? Well, most of the dancers stepped on them before I could pick them up for you." All that money and he couldn't even buy me some decent flowers for my birthday. (I hope that doesn't sound too stuck up.) Finally I had enough, and I wrote out a list of every reason that I had to dump him. It was around midnight when I called him (he was still awake), and I read off every item on the list. There were twelve or thirteen on there, and none of them repeated. I learned that Cute + Money + Nice Car does not equal a stable guy. There's more to someone than just their outer appearance.

—*Natalie*

Ronaldo was pretty damn sure that money made the world go round, and Daniel was positive that he was more important than your average taxi driver, based solely on his bottom line. But we all know neither of them was right. Mr. Rich is many things to us, but he's not the be-all and end-all. Neither is Mr. Macho, but what great fun we can have finding that out.

Been There, Learned This

○ You can enjoy the finer things in life, but you don't need them to survive.

○ Being with Mr. Rich and not worrying about money can make can realize you generally spend far too much time worrying about it.

○ Money can't buy you love—a nice dinner though, absolutely.

○ The rich really are different from you and me: money can destroy ambition, create unrealistic expectations, encourage self-centeredness, and generally get in the way of an authentic relationship.

A THERAPIST WEIGHS IN

One thing a woman can learn from dating a wealthy guy is that money is not salvation. It's easy to think that wealth is the answer. However, things often get more complicated with money. Rarely does it offer a rescue from life's problems.
—Eric Levin, Ph.D.
Philadelphia, Pennsylvania

Check Yourself Quiz
IS MR. RICH FOR YOU?

Answer "Yes" or "No" to each question. Then use the scoring section to check whether Mr. Rich is for you.

_____ 1. I can put my wallet back in my handbag when my date wields his gold Amex card without rolling my eyes or muttering, "Show-off."

_____ 2. I can get used to being showered with gifts.

_____ 3. I can turn my head and whistle a distracting tune when somebody acts as though money entitles him to more than the average Joe.

_____ 4. I can handle going to the symphony and then going back to my own less-than-palatial home.

_____ 5. I can shake off the calls of "gold digger!" from my friends.

_____ 6. I can quietly sit on the other end of the phone while my mother dreams of an easy retirement.

_____ 7. I wouldn't change a thing about my life for a minute, even if I had the chance.

_____ 8. If someone took me out for a fancy dinner and a show, I'd feel pressured to repay him—sexually if that's all I had.

_____ 9 I've always wondered how the other half lives.

_____ 10. I know just the guy, and I think he'd be amenable.

SCORING

1.	Yes: 1	No: 0		6.	Yes: 1	No: 0
2.	Yes: 1	No: 0		7.	Yes: 0	No: 1
3.	Yes: 1	No: 0		8.	Yes: 0	No: 1
4.	Yes: 1	No: 0		9.	Yes: 1	No: 0
5.	Yes: 1	No: 0		10.	Yes: 2	No: 0

0–5   Roll your eyes to your heart's delight: no Mr. Rich for you.

6–7   Let me see that necklace again. You could be convinced.

8–11   Mr. Rich is a Mister on your list.

SWF ISO RWM

If you're looking for one of those men who make up the power structure in this country and you're willing to do your homework, look no further than Professor Channa Newman's "Wealthy White Males" class at Point Park College in Pittsburgh, Pennsylvania. Newman's class explores the rich, white leaders of our century, how they rose to power and what impact their wealth and power have on the rest of us. Grades are based on two projects—one that researches any organization or hangout where the wealthy congregate and another than looks into the life and times of a rich, white man of your choice.

No word on whether you can get extra credit from dating an actual rich guy.

Russo, S. "Point Park College Prof. Teaches Course on 'Wealthy White Males.'" Accuracy in Academia Campus Report. [www.academia.org/campus_reports/2002/december_2002_4.html], Dec. 2002.

MR. RICHEST: BILL GATES

The richest guy in the world seems to have a permanent bunk on the *Forbes* "Richest" list—in 2002, he weighed in with over $50 billion.[2] If he were single, would you want to date Bill Gates?

PROS

○ When you go into a candy store, you are the proverbial kid in the candy store.

○ You could actually test the "Money makes the world go round" theory.

○ Do you need to get away? What island do you want to buy?

CONS

○ Just think of the junk mail and solicitations he must get. Is there even time to go out?

○ He has all that money, and he keeps giving himself that bowl haircut.

○ He's a college dropout. What does that say about his ambition?

Chapter

12

Mr. Macho

Mr. Macho had his heyday when the Village People sang "Macho, Macho Man," and his allure has been going steadily south since. (And even back then the band played the song for irony, giggling that they were far from traditionally "masculine.") *Macho* connotes a guy in tight jeans, wearing more jewelry than his girlfriend, strutting down the street. The thesaurus doesn't treat him much better. Synonyms for *macho* include "bluster, boasting, bombast, braggadocio, bragging, bullying, crowing, fancy talk, . . . grandiosity, guts, hot air, . . . pomposity, pretension, . . . self-glorification, storming, swaggering, swelling."[1]

YES, EVEN MR. MACHO

But even though I dislike bluster and bombast as much as the next girl, I also see the appeal of Mr. Macho as one of our Mr. Right Nows (you knew I would!).

He Gets the Job Done

Macho appeal shows up most often in car ads. A 2001 television ad for the Nissan Frontier touted the truck as a "3,172-pound can of whup-ass." (Interestingly, the French CEO of Nissan was not familiar with the American phrase *whup-ass*. But once it was decoded for him, he said "oui" to the ad.[2])

A Mister with whup-ass isn't just the guy you want to avoid in a dark alley; he's the guy who tells the cable company that *no,* you can't wait at home from 9 A.M. to 6 P.M. in the hope its installer will deign to drop by. He's the guy who insists at the restaurant—firmly but with that make-no-mistake-about-it voice—that *no,* the table by the kitchen near the screaming child *isn't* to your satisfaction. He's the guy who doesn't blink when the highway signs flash "Detour Ahead" and rain is falling in sheets from the blue-black sky.

He's All Man

Yes, we all know the appeal of the sensitive guy. But I'm talking now about the guy who, just by standing there with his big arms and straight talk, makes you feel more like a woman. Suddenly, you're more aware of your hair (and who the hell thinks about her hair, except when she's watching shampoo commercials where the hair acts like a stunt double, cascading off the shoulders in a way no normal hair ever could), of the way you can actually smile just a little, with just the tips of your full, red lips turning up. Before you know it, when you're around Mr. Macho your shoulders go back, and *bling!* there are your breasts. Who is this guy who makes you all too aware of the body you're coexisting with but haven't been dreamily floating inside of—till now?

He's all man. And guys feel pretty strongly about being considered all man. The State of Oregon understood this need when it went looking for more nurses. It launched a whup-ass ad campaign, with hard-jawed welder types challenged to be nurses, under the caption "Are you man enough to be a nurse?"[3] It was all about that ongoing debate: Can a man be a man (cue breasts to perk) and still be a nurse? Or a nursery school teacher or anything else even remotely touchy-feely?

There are many situations in which being a stereotypical male will get you nowhere, but it can get you pretty far if you're a Mr. Right Now.

He Gets The Job Done, in Bed, While Being All Man

See the chapter about Mr. Sex if you doubt the appeal of this one. One early 1990s indie film opens with a protracted sex scene. So long in fact that the heroine keeps checking the clock on the bedside table. She's frustrated with her sexy, Latin lover. What has he got to prove? She wonders and she keeps wondering until she has a romp with her boss, and he comes and goes before she even starts to rev up. She suddenly, agonizingly, sees the true importance of Mr. Macho.

MY MR. MACHO

I dated my Mr. Macho on an army base in Israel. I was just out of college and looking for an adventure. I found it on the base, where I and other similarly soft Americans volunteered among the macho for three weeks. Appreciating the appeal of Mr. Macho, the American girls paired off with soldiers, leaving the pasty American boys to play a lot of cards. My boyfriend for the duration was Giddy, an eighteen-year-old who looked pretty swell with a blowtorch in his hands.

Our first day on the base the manager divided us into groups. The girls were assigned to helping in the laundry or the office and the boys to fixing jeeps (*jeepeem* in Hebrew) with blowtorches and sharp implements. I would have none of that and raised my hand. "I'd like to work in the garage," I told the manager. A room full of Mr. Machos turned to regard me. I stared back.

Giddy showed me how to turn on the blowtorch, how to wield its hot blue light. I had to figure out the helmet myself because Giddy refused higher-ups' orders to wear one. I won the admiration of the other American girls by dating Giddy, earning inclusion in a pecking order I never cracked in high school. But in dating my Mr. Macho, I got more than that.

It wasn't Giddy's influence that pushed me to volunteer to work with fire in long sleeves and pants on a desert outpost in July. I've always felt that need to push myself, to prove my "feminist" fancy talk held more than words. But it was Giddy and his fellow soldiers—who clearly wondered when my strutting would tire me out—who kept me going. I even joined the all-male soccer team. I'm a horrible soccer player (I played "left bench" in high school), but I was smaller than the guys on this team and fast. I played after work in the garage, and when the games ran hours long and no one took a water break, neither did I. I became known on the adjoining base as "soccer girl." Once, when I ran an errand on that base, a soldier looked me up and down: "*You're* soccer girl?" he asked. Apparently he was expecting someone butchier or at least with a bit more height and heft to her. But he said it with respect.

It's not that everything about Mr. Macho is great. If it were, we'd still be seeing lots of men wearing shirts with the collars open so wide they touch the shoulders, all the better to display lots of chains and a hairy chest. Or at the very least we'd see more men who don't bridle at the title.

Even when Mr. Macho turns out to have a gooey center, it is, for better or worse, covered in a hard shell:

> Just picture a nice little Jewish girl dating a nice Mexican Catholic. All of the stereotypes were true in this guy's case. He was very protective yet territorial. He was also exceptionally romantic. He sent me on a scavenger hunt all over my college town to ask me to his fraternity's formal. The final stop was home and there were Hershey's kisses leading up the stairs. My room was covered in candy, flowers, balloons. I still have all of the clues in a scrap book.
>
> But boy did he get pissed if another guy looked at me.
>
> —*Maya*

And it's always possible that the hard shell is covering up more than you'd think:

I once dated this Navy guy who was all about how much of a man being in the Navy made him and how his uniform somehow meant that everyone needed to respect him above the "civilian" population. He was also into stereotypically macho things—like fixing cars and those motocross-type motorcycles and any kind of athletic competition—and he had to be the best and the winner of everything, even Pictionary. He'd also have a freak-out if any other guy even looked in my direction. He was more than willing to have a bar fight over any of the above.

But as an interesting side note—when we broke up, he stole all my (male) gay porn. Hmmm.

—Andrea

Playing with the really, truly Mr. Macho turns the mock axiom "It's only fun until someone loses an eye" into a real warning. Which, strangely, can be flattering:

After I started dating a boyfriend, he and his best friend got into a gigantic fight and almost stopped being friends (at least according to the rumor that got to me). At the time I was kind of shocked. I had no clue his best friend had an interest in me. Then I found it kind of funny.

Breaking up a friendship . . . over me? And then of course I was flattered that two guys wanted to date me and actually fought over me. How cool is that?

—Christy

But eventually enough is enough:

I dated a few Mr. Machos. They always wanted to fight, to hit something (not me, thank God). One broke his hand when he punched his truck. He dented the truck too. His injury affected the rest of his college football career. His thoughts on what he'd done? "At least it wasn't a person." They were all so annoying, constantly paranoid about people wanting to fight them when it wasn't the case. Now that I think about it, I never really saw a fight between two humans. Most of it was all talk, no action (unless you call punching a truck action).

Now I'm with a very passive, laid back, wouldn't-hurt-a-fly, rarely-gets-mad wonderful man.

—*Ruth*

Once again, dating one kind of Mister helps you see what you really want out of life.

Unless what you really want out of life is to change somebody. (Cue the dark mood music.) That's the thorn in the Mr. Macho bush: that terribly naïve idea of a (generally) young woman that she can be the one to save him from himself. Let me stop you right there: the Misters out there are about fun, sampling, and learning more about yourself. But as they say about scuba diving: leave only footprints, take only pictures. You can't change the landscape. People grow up in their own time, not on anyone else's urgent schedule. But if you're willing to accept the rules of this Mister and appreciate him, like the others, for what he is and don't try to make him into something he's not ready to be, he can be great fun and pretty cool for your ego.

Still, naysayers will pooh-pooh my love of Mr. Macho. They'll wonder why I can't handle the detour in the pouring rain all by myself. I'm perfectly aware that we women can get the job done ourselves. This doesn't diminish the appeal of a rough and tough Mr. Macho. It's not about diminishing our-selves (does Mr. Sex's prowess lessen our own?) but about appreciating the strengths in others. In this case, rugged, sexy others.

If you like Mr. Macho, you may be game for stepping a lit-tle farther out on that limb and dancing with Mr. Dangerous. Read on.

Been There, Learned This

○ It's cool to feel like the queen of the world (but there's no need for others to come to blows defending your title).

○ Guys tend to grow up and out of machismo, so you've got to act fast to get in on the fun.

○ A deep connection is grand, but sometimes all you need is a strut down the main drag on a Saturday night.

A THERAPIST WEIGHS IN

A macho-type man would most likely be someone who is highly independent with a strong sense of self. Therefore, he may be good for someone who has co-dependent tendencies and traits, since someone with these traits is looking for a partner that she can take care of and nurture. Thus, a macho-like man would not enable these detrimental tendencies.
—Leigh Heerema, MA in counseling
Bloomfield, New Jersey

Check Yourself Quiz
ARE YOU READY FOR MR. MACHO?

Answer "Yes" or "No" to each question. Then use the scoring section to check whether Mr. Macho is for you.

_____ 1. I'll fix my own damn carburetor, thank you.

_____ 2. My favorite movie is *Saturday Night Fever*.

_____ 3. I appreciate a man who'll kill anyone who looks at me funny.

_____ 4. Anybody can spray-paint my name on the side of a bridge. I want deep, honest communication.

_____ 5. I don't much like walking my dog late at night alone.

_____ 6. Real men walk away from fights.

_____ 7. It's faster to walk down the street with all that strutting.

_____ 8. Any man who says "my woman" gets kneed in the groin.

_____ 9. I like to find my boyfriends in the gym—preferably bench pressing more than I weigh.

_____ 10. I know just the guy, and I think he'd be amenable.

SCORING

1.	Yes: 0	No: 1	6.	Yes: 0	No: 1
2.	Yes: 1	No: 0	7.	Yes: 0	No: 1
3.	Yes: 1	No: 0	8.	Yes: 0	No: 1
4.	Yes: 0	No: 1	9.	Yes: 1	No: 0
5.	Yes: 1	No: 0	10.	Yes: 2	No: 0

0–5   You need somebody a little more sensitive than Mr. Macho cares to be.

6–7   You could consider cozying up to Mr. Macho.

8–11   He's all man and he's all yours.

WHO, ME? SCARED?

According to a Purdue University study, men want us to think they're fearless. Researchers asked men and women how scared they were of fish, rats, mice, and roller-coasters. Men pretty much scoffed at the question. Then the groups were asked to watch short movies about fish, rats, mice, and roller-coasters. This time, they were told that their heart rates were being monitored (though they weren't), so their fear levels could be measured. When men thought their fears were being electronically captured, they copped to feeling more scared than they had previously admitted. Women seemed more hon-est, reporting the same levels of fear whether or not they thought their levels were being measured.

The conclusion? Looks like men fear fish, rats, mice, and roller-coasters more than they let on. And they're not too fond of being caught lying either.

Sounds pretty macho to me.

"Macho Man: Men Afraid to Admit They're Afraid." HealthDayNews, [www.hon.ch/News/HSN/513546.html], 2003.

MR. MOST MACHO:
ARNOLD SCHWARZENEGGER

The quintessential Mr. Macho is Ahhhhnold "Hasta la vista, Baby" Schwarzenegger. In the passenger seat of his Hummer, you're untouchable. Would you want to date the terminator?

PROS

- No need to fret if you ever find yourself pinned under an SUV.
- Whenever he leaves, you know he'll "be back."
- As First Lady of California, you'll get some macho body-guards too.

CONS

- You can't understand 90 percent of what he's saying.
- He has *Total [California] Recall* notoriety.
- You'll have to deal with the Kennedys.

Chapter

13

Mr. Dangerous

. . . So they were carried off as
Marriage bed plunder: even so, many continued
To make panic look fetching. Any girl who resisted her
    pursuer
Too vigorously would find herself picked up
And borne off regardless. "Why spoil those pretty eyes with
    weeping?"
She'd hear, "I'll be all to you
That your Dad ever was to your Mum."

—Ovid, *Art of Love*

Women have always swooned for the bad boy. Men in spurs faced off on deserted, dusty streets, declaring that the town wasn't big enough for the two of them, and women in hoopskirts watched it happen from behind swinging saloon doors. Mothers are forever warning their daughters away from the guy with the knowing half-smile, and girls are forever turning their heads and smiling back at him. Two thousand years before I was shivering over the boys in *The Outsiders* and tacking a poster of Ralph Macchio to the inside of my closet, Ovid was penning poetry about the phenomenon of Mr. Dangerous.

That's because he's notorious, sexy, and so fun. He's about living outside the parameters of your own life and taking chances (even if only by watching the chances he takes). With Mr. Dangerous you run with the wolves for a bit. I have and it's a wonderful feeling. Although I've never put myself in harm's way (unless riding on the back of a motorcycle counts), I've tasted the freedom, the badness, the thrilling danger in boys all but tattooed with "Mr. Dangerous" across their biceps.

> He was fun. He opened my eyes to the "real world" and my wild side. I was so desperate to allow that side of me out. To let my hair down and be wild and spontaneous, because that is who I am.
>
> —*Hope*

THE ATTRACTION OF DANGER

Mr. Dangerous serves one of three purposes in our romantic journey.

Explore the Precarious

Because he takes ownership of the danger and any disapproval, we can learn about our own wild side in relative safety.

I liked that he was dangerous and edgy and so successful. I liked how different he was from most of the guys I dated: the stories he told, the way people listened to him, the way I felt when I was with him.

—*Jane*

He was totally not the type for me. He was the "bad kid"—did drugs (though not when I was with him, I think), had lots of sex (not with me), skipped class, couldn't pass the classes he did attend, drove fast, drank, smoked, drove fast while drinking and smoking . . . all the things that would make my mother pass out if I told her. He had a bad boy cuteness about him that was really attractive.

I really saw myself change when I was with him. He did bring me out of my shell to some extent, though. Here I am, the goody-goody eighteen-year-old virgin and he's this rebel bad kid who actually had a kid on the way with another girl while we were dating. He was rough around the edges and it rubbed off on me. I started to think differently when I was around him and say things that I never thought I would. I actually smoked a few times that semester (cigarettes only), something I'd never done and never did again.

Looking back, I realize I liked him because I was tired of being that goody-goody and I wanted a change.

—*Natalie*

One Mr. Dangerous of mine, tattooed, motorcycle-riding Benny, threw wild and not-altogether-legal parties in college and slept with a certain rock star whenever she came to town. I didn't quite understand the appeal of either behavior—the idea of over-the-top parties got old quick, and being one of many rock groupies didn't seem very fun—but that didn't mean I shied away from his crazy stories. I wanted to warm my hands by this fire, but not set them blazing.

And sometimes we come a bit too close to the fire. Gayle slept with her married college professor. Understanding the irony, she admitted he "encouraged" her writing even as he brought her morals way down. She saw the "poor ethics" of the situation, but "wanted him anyway." Although she hopes she got it out of her system, she learned the surprising truth about herself and what she was "capable of."

Courting danger allows us to try out the dangerous parts of ourselves through someone else. When we don't approve of these parts, "it's easier to have them exist in the boyfriend," says therapist Deborah Shelkrot Permut. "If dating is approached as a series of experiences that the woman has which can be fun or painful or enjoyable, but which reveal things about herself, the dangerous boyfriend is a great experience to have."

My point exactly!

He Allows Us to Explore Our Limits— and Decide How Far Is Too Far

Anna Rosner, whose research I described in Chapter Two, finds that much of literature hammers home the lesson that a woman is smart "to recognize the potential for unhappiness" with a dangerous partner. Bélasire, the heroine of Madame de La Fayette's *Zayde* (1670), for example, falls in love with the handsome Alphonse. He proves to be "violently jealous and volatile," says Rosner, and the desperately unhappy Bélasire realizes that their union can lead only to further misery. She decides not to marry Alphonse (she believes she was "born with an aversion to marriage" anyway) and retires to a nunnery.

"Remember me," she tells Alphonse, "and wish, for my serenity, that I never remember you."[1]

In real life Sarah also figured out her limits by dating a Mr. Dangerous:

He had an exciting job and took me to parties with famous people. He was cute, sweet, loving, generous even when he did not have enough for himself. I became more into partying than him, and eventually we both had to go into recovery for addiction. That was the end of my old life, and the beginning of my life as it is now, which is great. At the time, I was addicted to excitement. I wanted to not look at my own problems so I could blame things on his drug addiction. But jeez, those hangovers and nosebleeds! Now I've learned I am worth . . . treating myself and those around me with my best intentions and with my clear mind.

It's a Power Trip—Maybe We Can Change Him

This scenario succeeds only in fairy tales. Anna Rosner has found many such stories in which love and marriage transforms the dangerous man into a good one, thereby sending a message to the young female reader:

Many of the male partners are originally somewhat dangerous; the Beast, for example, in *Beauty and the Beast.* He is an interesting character in that his later acceptance by Beauty reveals a very clear lesson to young women: you must accept your husband, warts and all, and doing so will lead to your subsequent "reward" (the transformation from Beast to Prince). It's essential to remember that most young aristocratic women were forced into unhappy but financially beneficial unions with men far beyond them in age and experience.[2]

But, alas, life isn't a fairy tale. In real life we usually find out the opposite is true—you can't change anyone—a valuable lesson in itself:

He experimented with drugs and he ran with a fast crowd. He was underage and drank all the time too. He was *extremely* smart, but his maturity level was practically nonexistent, except when it came to having a girlfriend. He really did have genuine feelings for me. However, he didn't bring out the best in me. He also made me act cooler than I was. I was acting to be like him and fit in with his friends. I wasn't being myself.

He was the first "bad boy" I ever dated. Before him I only dated the "clean-cut" types of guys. I wanted to see what a bad boy was like. I enjoyed the sex and the excitement of being with a bad boy. I liked other people we worked with knowing that we were together. The other girls were so jealous I was with him!

Then I literally caught him cheating on me. I went to visit him at work, but I didn't know he was off that day. When I got to the store, he was walking by with his other girlfriend when I ran into both of them. It was such a showdown when I told him off and said it was over, right in front of her. Boy, I hope she dropped him like a hot potato.

From my relationship with him I learned not to ever change because of a boyfriend. If you don't approve of their behavior (if it's drugs, alcohol, and so on), voice your opinion. If he doesn't respect your feelings and opinions, ditch him. I also found out that I am capable of accepting a person for who they are—he was a drinker and used drugs occasionally. I accepted that when I was with him. I recognized early on that you can't change someone. If they want to change they will, but you can't control what they do.

—*Mandy*

He was everything I'd never dated before. He was someone parents and friends warned you against. He seemed deep and mysterious. I see now that he was a quitter. He never finished anything. Our relationship ended when he left the country without telling me. He dropped out of three different colleges. He never completed anything. The relationship taught me that I am susceptible to images. I learned to dig beyond the façade in order to trust the person I was with.

—*Nancy*

Dating Mr. Dangerous works best when you're interested in strolling in the dangerous neighborhood but not up for buying your own house there. It's safer to hold his hand when exploring, and it's exciting, and it's yet another way to find out about ourselves. It's good to know how much of a dark side we've got, if only to better understand our own boundaries.

DANGEROUS, NOT STUPID

Marianne Williamson tells us: "Many women . . . are stuck in a place that is dangerous but seductive. They want desperately to get out of the pattern but . . . [t]hey lack the self-esteem to save their own lives, so they repeatedly form relationships which are basically wrong for them."[3] I'm all for heeding Williamson's call to avoid the secretly married men who lead you on, seduce you, and leave you; the parasites, predators, and con men; the self-destructive obsessive gamblers, alcoholics, and drug addicts; the brutes, the jerks, and momma's boys.

But there's a distinction to be made here. There's plain old pain and there's thrilling danger. Modern self-help writers often don't distinguish between the two and want to warn us away from all dangerous boys. I'm siding here with the ancient poet Ovid, who knows that sometimes she doth protest too much. I'm not talking about the jerks when I ask you to consider Mr. Dangerous. I'm talking about the guys who live life a little faster than you or I might ever dare.

Dating Mr. Dangerous is about experiencing the thrill of the forbidden. I've got a bit more of the forbidden for you: Mr. Sex.

Been There, Learned This

- Mr. Dangerous can keep the element of danger, of being off-kilter, alive in us. As novelist Kurt Vonnegut said, "Out on the edge you see all the kinds of things you can't see from the center." I remember what it felt like to speed down the highway on the back of a motorcycle and try to always keep the wind in my hair.

- There are times when we need Mr. Dangerous to take the fallout for "crazy" ideas and adventures, and there's a time when I want to take it myself. So I trek to the border of China alone, and take full credit for the idea.

○ Life isn't a fairy tale. If he looks like the Beast, we must accept that he's no Beauty.

A THERAPIST WEIGHS IN

Dating a dangerous guy is exciting. A woman may feel she's always been the good girl, and she's tired of conforming. Dating him helps her take risks she may never have thought of taking on her own but always wanted to experience. But marrying Mr. Dangerous is often a really bad idea because she's rebelling. She's saying to her parents: "I don't have to listen to you. I make my own choices." What she has to figure out is whether he's a serious rebellion or a reflection of who and what she is.
—Ruth Greer, Ph.D.
Rye, New York

Check Yourself Quiz
IS MR. DANGEROUS FOR YOU?

Answer "Yes" or "No" to each question. Then use the scoring section to check whether Mr. Dangerous is for you.

_____ 1. I want to ride a motorcycle; I just don't want to *own* a motorcycle.

_____ 2. I've always had a secret thing for blue-haired guys.

_____ 3. I like to know where my guy is at all times.

_____ 4. I like to bring my boyfriends home—so he'd have to take out his earring and cover up his tattoos, but otherwise I'm into it.

_____ 5. I admit it: I'm extremely judgmental.

_____ 6. I've always been a sit-on-the-sidelines kind of girl, and I'm tired of it.

_____ 7. I know he doesn't *look* like he has a softer side—but I'd like to try to find it.

_____ 8. I'm ambivalent about bungee jumping: sometimes it looks like fun and sometimes it just looks stupid.

_____ 9. My last boyfriend wore chinos every day of his life.

_____ 10. I know just the guy, and I think he'd be amenable.

SCORING

1.	Yes: 1	No: 0	6.	Yes: 1	No: 0
2.	Yes: 1	No: 0	7.	Yes: 1	No: 0
3.	Yes: 0	No: 1	8.	Yes: 1	No: 0
4.	Yes: 0	No: 1	9.	Yes: 1	No: 0
5.	Yes: 0	No: 1	10.	Yes: 2	No: 0

0–5   Stick with the chinos guy.

6–7   You could let down your hair if you tried.

8–11   Gentlemen, start your motorcycle engines; she's ready for Mr. Dangerous.

THE DANGEROUS WAY OUT

The *American Journal of Public Health* reports that at every age, men are in poorer health than women and have a higher death rate. One of the reasons for this is men's propensity for danger. Compared to women, men die twice as often as a result of homicide, suicide, and accidents. When some good sense could forestall the Grim Reaper, men often prefer the dangerous way out. They drink more, for instance, and suffer twice the rate of cirrhosis of the liver because of it.

Men are more likely than women to work dangerous jobs. And more likely to just do something stupid. Think of all the worst college pranks you've ever heard of. It wasn't members of sororities who stole their pledges' clothing and then dropped the kids off in high-crime neighborhoods in the dead of night.

There's dangerous, and there's stupid. Turns out, men are more often both.

Williams, D. R. "The Health of Men: Structured Inequalities and Opportunities." *American Journal of Public Health,* May 2003, 93(5), 724–731.

MR. MOST DANGEROUS:
ANTONIO BANDERAS

In the 1995 hit *Desperado*, Antonio Banderas was just a strolling mariachi till a drug dealer smote his girlfriend. Next thing you know, he's packing a huge gun and out for revenge on dusty streets and in seedy bars, personal safety be damned. Would you want to be his new inamorata?

PROS
- When the killing is over, he'll play music for you.
- Smoldering doesn't refer just to the hot gun.
- Look at the size of that gun!

CONS
- You can't be squeamish: a lot of blood comes with his territory.
- It's difficult to make plans when he's got killing to do.
- You'll spend a lot of time in bars.

Chapter

14

Mr. Sex

And sometimes, what you need is sex—the potency, the power, the connection, the release. I once read a study that purported that the people who enjoy sex the most are married Christian women. I have no doubt it's because they feel strongly that they are doing God's most delicious work in the bed He's blessed.

My beds haven't always been so blessed, but I'm not complaining. I wouldn't call myself a mattress-hopper, but when I was ready to have sex, I explored and giggled and romped. It was a brand-new way of expressing myself with someone, and led to a new way of being desired, appreciated, understood.

It was also a great way to learn about both the vast expanse and ultimate limits of my own desire, sensuality, capacity for physical intimacy, and ability to let go.

THE THERAPEUTIC VALUE

Sometimes sex is just what the doctor ordered, especially after an emotionally bruising heartbreak. My friend Linda knew I'd understand her story:

I was friends with Tim for two years, during which I dated, moved in with, got engaged to, planned a wedding with, and broke up with another man. During all that time, Tim was watching me, hoping, and I knew it. A few days after Paul and I called it off, Tim called me.

"If you need a rebound, I'm here," he joked.

We talked about it. E-mailed back and forth. I told him, "I look fully baked, but I'm gooey inside."

I retreated for months before I was ready. And then he came to my house and cooked me a three-course dinner, and I felt the sudden urge to show off the dress I had just bought for a friend's wedding. I left the room and stepped back in wearing the body-hugging black dress. The edges of the back were trimmed in hot pink. The rest of the back was bare. He couldn't take his eyes off me.

"Turn around," he said, and I gave him a little twirl. He stood mute.

"Do you like it?" I goaded.

"You have no idea," he choked.

[Fade to black.]

CONTROVERSY OR GOOD FUN

Welcome to the most controversial of the Misters: Mr. Sex. Have your tomatoes and rotten eggs ready, Pat Robertson and Phyllis Schlafly. I've been converted, and you're going to need some well-aimed splattering food or a long hook to get me off my soapbox. I read with great interest Wendy Shalit's fascinating book *A Return to Modesty: Discovering the Lost Virtue.* Shalit hews to a strong line: premarital sex is to be avoided, and in a larger context, date rape, self-cutting, and anorexia can be cured by modesty of dress, behavior, and self. (In all cases, it's women who have to hold back; men will learn by their example.) Women don't really want sex without commitment, Shalit says; when they do have it, they're just giving in to make men happy and to make other, "badder" girls stop whispering about the modest girl's "issues."

"A young woman today has basically two options open to her: to pretend she's a man, or be feminine in a desperate, victim-like way," says Shalit.[1] I agree with many of Shalit's points—it can be very, very sexy to wait for sex, and teenage girls can only benefit from catering to their own needs and not those of hormone-infused boyfriends—but I disagree on this one. Wendy, women want sex too. I don't agree that sex education and talk of sex and, gasp, having sex, are the causes of all the evil in the world. I believe in dating Mr. Sex every once in a while, to remember your sexiness, explore your sensuality, declare your lust, hone your repertoire, and enjoy yourself—no strings attached. Something more than every once in a while is a lifestyle choice. Something less is another. But for many Mizzes, every once in a while is just right.

Mr. Sex doesn't have to be smart; he doesn't have to call tomorrow. He's not going to hang out with your friends, you're sure as hell not taking him home to meet your parents, and the conversation is never to include talk of the future. Isabelle knows what I mean:

He was a lifeguard. The first time I met him in person, there weren't any major sparks. He wasn't drop-dead gorgeous. He was just your average nice guy. One night, after going out with friends, we ended up going home together. Our brief (two months) relationship was only about sex. He was a nice guy. In fact we probably could have dated long term had we tried. That just wasn't what we were look-ing for from each other. He came along at a very low point in my life—I had just broken up with my fiancé, and I was feeling less than desirable. Being wanted and desired sexually was just what I needed.

Some might find such a relationship to be lacking, but I found it to be one of the most fulfilling of my life. He made me feel confi-dent about myself. He told me I was beautiful. He told me he want-ed me. I knew why he wanted me, and it felt damn good.

Those of us who have enjoyed a Mr. Sex wax rhapsodic about the experience—and not just about the sex.

He brought out my sexually adventurous side.

He made me a better dancer and a more adventurous person out-side the bedroom, less shy.

It's really simple when you look at it as Beth did:

We never really dated. We had been friends for many years. It was a time in my life when I did not want a relationship. He didn't want one either. It worked out well. He was, ahem, well-endowed. We had hot sex. Probably the best sex I have ever had in my whole life. The joy of the relationship? The orgasms. There was no agony. Though we no longer have sex, we are still friends. Sometimes it is fun to have sex with someone you have no emotional ties to. You can just enjoy the act. You don't have to agonize over daily relationship problems. It is just sex and that's it.

SEX AS FREEDOM

Mr. Sex is about fun, pleasure, and empowerment. And enjoying him is quite new to our history. In the tenth century, women retreated to nunneries to avoid marriage. By declaring themselves above the sexual fray, they "gained an almost mystical power from their . . . status."[2] Fast forward about a thousand years and now we can refuse—or delay—marriage, and sex can be *part* of our freedom to concentrate on ourselves.

And what a delicious freedom:

He looked just like Pierce Brosnan when he was younger. People used to stare at him on the street (my mother included). He was rather a bit of a morality-free zone. I don't think he ever had a girlfriend he didn't cheat on. I was pretty sure that since he was willing to cheat on someone with me he would be willing to cheat on me with someone else. I realized that the pretty package was all he had to offer and that I needed more. But at the time, we had a consistently amazing sexual relationship, and I still think Pierce Brosnan is hot.

—*Ingrid*

SOW YOUR OATS

Marriage among the young is often a product of the idealized desire to have sex only in the marital bed, supported by the confines and stability of marriage. This can lead to premature wedding bells, marriage just for the sake of getting into bed. Many if not most of twenty- and thirty-something women today are having sex (well, not this *minute*, but before marriage). We love it. We've got needs too (when you're not marrying at nineteen, the wait for marriage can be l-o-n-g), and satisfying those needs is not something we feel we need to defend.

Or is it? Although nearly every unmarried woman I know is sleeping with her boyfriend, we're all quick to point out how much we care for the guy or how he's seeing only us or how we've "never felt this way before." We're still hedging our bets. We don't sleep with every guy we date, and we look down our noses at those who do. We hold tight to double standards—any guy, given the chance, will sleep around—but we, not quite pure but definitely not tainted, have sex only in committed relationships.

But Julie knew what she wanted. Her Mr. Sex simply wouldn't have made the right husband:

> We knew each other for two years before anything happened. We work together (but in different departments). He drives me crazy (in a good way). We are totally attracted to each other and it works for both of us, considering our hectic schedules. He tells me how beautiful I am. Even the things I see as flaws, he loves about me. He makes me feel sexy, attractive, desirable—physically and in turn emotionally better about myself. Our relationship is physical. He is a

wonderful person, and one day some woman will be very lucky to have him. But I don't see him in my long-term future.

How many times has this happened to you? You weren't sure how much you liked the guy, but you knew you were attracted to him. Things got physical, and suddenly he's your boyfriend. Because, after all, only guys sow their wild oats. Women have sex with men who are their partners in deep, committed relationships—unless they're characters in *Sex and the City,* and even then they often worry about it (unless they're Samantha, the guy-like member of the quartet).

Well, how about if we acted a little like guys? What if we stopped thinking like Hope, who enjoyed her Mr. Sex but then, chastened by the voices in her head, declared, "I'm not that type of girl"? What if we refused to make sex about power (male) and victims (female)? What if we chose to strip sex of all that power and just . . . strip?

What if when it doesn't work out, we just get dressed and leave?

I was out with my friends at a bar when this guy walked up. He obviously knew my friends but hadn't met me. He sat down next to me to talk. He was a little older than me, always laughing, gorgeous dark skin and features, smart, funny, overall wonderful. We must have talked for over an hour. He took my number and called me about a week later to go out with his friends. We had a great time and ended up back at his place. One thing led to another, and pretty soon we were spending every night together. He was amazing in bed, and that's where we spent most of our time together. He definitely brought out something in me.

—*Tina*

When we look at Mr. Sex this way, he becomes just another Mister—another experience in life. No judgments, no lightning bolts crashing down on your head. Liberating, isn't it?

THREATENING MARRIAGE?

To really enjoy Mr. Sex (and you can take the quiz at the end of the chapter to see if you would), you need to reject the moralistic musings of others.

Danielle Crittendon, the author of *What Our Mothers Didn't Tell Us: Why Happiness Eludes the Modern Woman,* wants to scare us away from Mr. Sex and right into the marital bed. "[I]f women don't settle down at the same time as their friends," she warns us, "if we insist on our right to lead sexually unconstrained lives into our thirties and beyond, then we have to accept that there will be consequences to the long-term stability of *all* marriages, and even to our own ability to marry."[3] But I argue that it's just the opposite—it's those who constrain their sexual lives from an early age who run the risk of getting their kicks outside the marital bed, outside the institution of marriage. (As Mae West once said, "Marriage is a great institution. But I'm not ready for an institution.") I'll go so far as to say that enjoying Mr. Sex now will strengthen your marriage to a different Mister later.

Writer Scott Stossel makes a fascinating point worth recalling when disapproving scoldings bring you down:

> What conservatives . . . want is less a curb on sexual excess than a rolling back of the political gains that

women . . . have won under the auspices of the sexual revolution. [To demonstrate that loose morals wreak havoc] first, point out that sexual liberation had a tangible, "science"-based cost: AIDS and other STDs. Next, cast the net more widely so that if sexual liberation was associated with women's liberation, for example, and sexual liberation caused AIDS, then women's liberation caused AIDS. All forms of liberation and political change connected to the sixties and seventies get implicated in this way. Women's rights, gay rights, a woman's right to choose, and the freedom to do what you like in the privacy of your own bedroom all get thrown out the window with the bathwater.[4]

PROCEED WITH CAUTION

We know women's liberation didn't cause AIDS, but we must be responsible for our own welfare. Mr. Sex is a pleasure that should be reserved for a mature palate—and a woman in tune with the importance of protecting herself, physically and emotionally. For your Mr. Sex you may choose a man who isn't your best friend, so it's crucial not to lull yourself into believing he's going to have your best interests at heart. Sex is like the strongest cocktail—it can fool us into believing we're in love or we're immortal. Enjoy yourself, but keep your wits about you. Unfortunately, some women haven't:

He was a friend of a friend from a different college. He got me really drunk and stoned at a party and took me home with him. I think we dated for about a month or maybe six weeks long distance. I only saw him maybe five times total, usually just to drink and have sex. I knew he wasn't what I was looking for, but I was enjoying it while it lasted. Four months later, I was diagnosed with an STD.

—*Vera*

The sex was good. He was a good kisser, he was cute, and he had the most amazing blue eyes I've ever seen. But I have a lot of painful memories of that relationship, as it resulted in an unplanned and unwanted pregnancy.

—*Rose*

Vera's story is a cautionary tale for several reasons. Sex with a Mister should be fun for both of you and *always* be safe. Part and parcel of enjoying the Misters is taking care of your needs. If it takes drugs or alcohol to make him look like a good bet, he's not. And always, always use condoms. Being with Mr. Sex is about empowerment and sexuality. It's not about cringing the morning after. Rose suffered from her Mr. Sex physically and emotionally. This experience should not be about feeling the pleasure and disregarding the pain— you've got to take precautions, and you also need to figure out if Mr. Sex is right for you before you dive in.

I'm not pushing you into a relationship with any kind of Mister if it doesn't feel right to you. Enjoy those Misters you want, with your eyes open to the possible dangers, and *always* practice safe sex.

All the Misters have their strengths. Mr. Sex is great for staying up all night. Mr. Perfect Breakup is just what you need so you can sleep through the night—alone.

Been There, Learned This

○ Sometimes we need a no-strings relationship that is only about physical pleasure and creates no pressure for emotional depth and long-term commitment.

○ There's beauty in sex—and even good girls can benefit.

○ Good sex doesn't mean the rest of the relationship is golden. Sometimes separating sex out from emotions can keep us from staying involved longer than we should be.

○ Everything we choose to do, we should choose to do safely. Deciding to have a purely sexual relationship isn't an excuse for acting immaturely.

A THERAPIST WEIGHS IN

Very often women spend so much time looking for The Guy that they miss out on a lot, including sexual experiences for themselves. Many women don't understand they can have wonderful sex with men without the relationship "going" anywhere—it's just great sex. Too many women romanticize sex—if the sex is there, they think something else has got to be there. I see that over and over and over again. But it just means it's great sex and that's all it is and all it's ever going to be. Sure you want to meet a man and have great sex and intelligent conversation and support. But what about in the meantime?
—Jennie Ackerman, CSWR
New York, New York

Check Yourself Quiz:
IS MR. SEX FOR YOU?

Answer "Yes" or "No" to each question. Then use the scoring section to check whether Mr. Sex is for you.

_____ 1. I enjoy sex.

_____ 2. I can handle a no-strings relationship. I realize he's really *not* going to call me in the morning to say what a great time he had.

_____ 3. I want to be uninhibited.

_____ 4. Sometimes I want to be desired purely for my body.

_____ 5. I fear being objectified.

_____ 6. I find sex without a surrounding relationship empty and unsatisfying.

_____ 7. I'm deathly afraid of STDs like herpes and, God forbid, AIDS, and don't trust that a condom is going to keep me safe all the time.

_____ 8. I'm deathly afraid of getting pregnant accidentally.

_____ 9. I get very attached to a man emotionally when I sleep with him.

_____ 10. I know just the guy, and I think he'd be amenable.

1.	Yes: 1	No: 0	6.	Yes: 0	No: 1
2.	Yes: 1	No: 0	7.	Yes: 0	No: 1
3.	Yes: 1	No: 0	8.	Yes: 0	No: 1
4.	Yes: 1	No: 0	9.	Yes: 0	No: 1
5.	Yes: 0	No: 1	10.	Yes: 2	No: 0

SCORING

0–5   Stay on your side of the bed—Mr. Sex is not for you.

6–7   Think about it carefully. With your head.

8–11   Close the door and go for it!

FIND MR. SEX AND CALL ME IN THE MORNING

What can sex do? Various studies tout all manner of excellent bed remedies. Studies say sex

○   Cures headaches

○   Promotes blood flow

○   Helps you relax

○   Wards off colds and flu

○   Reduces pain

○   Lessens cramps

Sounds like Mr. Sex is more of a necessity than a perk.

MR. SEXIEST: COLIN FARRELL

Colin Farrell, the cursing, smoking, drinking Irish actor, holds nothing back. In his usual salty language he told *Playboy* magazine how very much he believes in casual sex. Basically, he told his interviewer, if it feels so good, how can it be bad?[5] Is Colin Farrell worth the night?

PROS
- He's not going to propose. His one marriage, at age nineteen, lasted a mere four months and he never looked back. So when he says it's all for fun, he's not blowing smoke.
- He takes his casual sex very seriously, so you can only benefit.
- Whom he kisses makes big news, so your public display of affection could land you some prime space in the tabloids.

CONS
- He curses like a sailor.
- It's entirely possible he likes his beer and cigarettes more than he likes his women.
- Though he told *Playboy* he's all for condoms, he apparently forgets his own advice: a former girlfriend is having his (first) baby.

Chapter

15

Mr. Perfect Breakup

With all of this dating, breaking up is going to be inevitable. And just as there is good, healthy, fun dating, there is good, healthy, fun breaking up. Well, OK, breakups may not be fun, but think about it: breakups should entail a coming apart that makes sense and feels right. Sure, when most of us think of breaking up, we also automatically think of the ugly aftermath—tears, insomnia, the repeated refrain of "Why? Why? Why?"—that comes from uncertainty, loneliness, and fear. But really, not all breakups need to be horrible. Sometimes, if you let them, they can be *perfect*, or at least a great relief, allowing you to walk away from a Mister with a better sense of yourself, with your pride preserved—and best of all, with no bitterness or hard feelings toward the guy.

"Is there really such a thing . . . as a perfect breakup after fourth grade?" Jane countered when I asked for her good breakup stories. Ingrid said, "I have *always* cried when I broke up with someone. It's like a visceral reaction to the words, 'I can't see you anymore.'" Ingrid's reaction makes sense, and it's our usual one to breaking up. But sometimes when we break up, all the pieces fall into place and we feel *right*. Sarah knew this feeling, and it helped her call an end to a relationship that could have just kept dragging along:

> We were together six months. He was cute, sweet, attentive, fun, and dumb as a box of rocks. We watched a movie and he just kept asking questions about the plot. He did not understand what was going on. It could have been *Top Gun* for all I remember, but he just could not get it. I finally said I didn't feel that I wanted to continue being with him, that there were other women who would really appreciate him and I was not doing him justice by being with him. We are still friends, and the guys I date now have to be very intelligent.

Jesse was on the receiving end of a breakup, but she hardly felt dumped. When it's done honestly, kindly, and quickly, breaking up can actually be refreshing:

> We met at a bar we both danced at. He was pretty fearless socially (he used to walk up and down the bar offering everyone a stick of gum, just for fun), so that helped me to become more outgoing. He encouraged a girl he didn't know to stop practicing her dancing on the sidelines and join us on the dance floor. He broke up with me

over the phone. He said "You know I like you, and I know we've agreed to be exclusive, but I have to tell you because I wouldn't feel right if I didn't. I like your best friend. I'm sorry, it's not something I can help, but I wanted to be honest with you."

FACING UP TO BREAKING UP

My single friends and I have an ongoing double standard, and it works like this. When a guy just stops calling, we're pissed. We think he should at least have had the decency to phone and tell us he doesn't want to go out again! But when the shoe's on the other foot, and he's calling and we're just not interested, we let our answering machines pick up. The fact is, nobody likes rejection—whether you're rejecting somebody or you're the one getting the heave-ho. But think how much better it would be if everybody had the maturity of Jesse's Mr. Perfect Breakup: "Oh, well, that makes sense," we'd think as we heard him out. And that would be that.

My mom used to call me The World's Worst Breaker-Upper. It didn't matter that a relationship had clearly run its course; I hemmed and hawed and made myself miserable. When a guy split with me, I'd cry, even if just five minutes ago I had been wishing our relationship were over. I always blamed myself and was suddenly smacked between the eyes with precious memories of the good times (and if the good times were few, the tape just kept repeating the same couple of scenes). I never stopped to face the painfully obvious: in every dating situation that doesn't end in marriage, breaking up is inevitable. It's happened before and it's definitely going to happen again. Instead of sighing with relief and taking to heart my father's wise comment—"If it ends, it's supposed to end"—I would regret things I had said or done, and wish I could take back that last time I threw my hands up in frustration and stomped out the door. Breakups happen, they're normal, and there's so much to learn from them, but I foolishly focused on ways I might have somehow saved our hole-riddled ship, even as we were neck-deep in cold water.

I joke that if you want to become a breezy breaker-upper, go through a broken engagement. As I tell people about life after calling it off: once you've pulled your engagement ring off your finger, left it for him on the bed you once shared, and walked out of the house you once jointly owned, dating breakups are a walk in the park.

I'M STILL STANDING

Healthy, even perfect breakups require a little dance that goes something like this:

1. Acknowledge the good points of the relationship, and accept that the bad ones outweigh them, which leads nicely to the next step . . .

2. Realize that the two of you have no future. The jig is up.

3. Take some time to accept your part in the relationship's demise.

4. When that time is up, approach your soon-to-be ex.

5. Break up with him: nicely, firmly, with minimum sentimentality and no loopholes offered. Leave out clichéd (even if true) excuses such as: "It's not you, it's me,"

"You deserve someone who can love you like you deserve to be loved," and "We can still be friends."

6. Do, however, leave the door open to future friendship.

7. Do not backslide (that means no "thanks for the memories" sex).

Just as dating helps you better understand yourself, so does breaking up. And I eventually discovered that I could survive breaking up. I didn't die. I didn't fall apart. I made it through. That may seem obvious to those among us who aren't hysterical breaker-uppers, but it is an important epiphany for those of us who find cold comfort in a carton of Häagen-Dazs the night(s) after the final good-bye. Many women have a visceral reaction to saying good-bye, a chemical reaction to not having that Mister around anymore that threatens their sanity.

What I finally realized after my fiancé Mark called it off was that I was still standing. Call it maturity, call it just simply letting go, but it worked for me. In her song "Thank U," Alanis Morissette tells us about the way the very act of deciding you don't need something brings that elusive peace straight to your door. It's nothing less than a Zen "Aha!" moment. Others have felt it too:

I realized that people cannot be changed, no matter how much you want them to. You have to deal with a person just how they are, and they will fight you to no end if you try to change them. So when he called me at three A.M. to talk and we ended up breaking it off, it was OK, it really was. It was for the best and we both agreed. There was just nothing there for either of us.

—Natalie

Which doesn't mean the breakup's completely painless for everyone involved. It just means it's right, as Vera can attest. And that's a lot.

> We were good friends before we started dating. We could talk for
> hours about nothing. He probably was a lot of what I was looking
> for, but I fell in love with another guy. I had my new boyfriend break
> up with him. They were visiting each other and I had the new one
> tell this one that we were going to start dating. Not my best logisti-
> cal plan, but it worked. We all stayed friends after with (I think) not
> too much animosity. We are all actually still friends. I broke up with
> him the wrong way, but it was right to break up. He was annoyed at
> first, but he got it too. In that experience I realized the importance
> of being really good friends. It can carry you into and out of a
> romantic relationship without destroying the friendship.

IT'S REALLY *NOT* YOU—IT'S ME

In fact, I'll go out on a limb here and say it's not usually about him. My own perfect breakup started with what I thought would be a great relationship. I met Evan on-line, and we had a middling first date; he had recently been transferred from New York City and was pining for it. I came home from the first date knowing nothing about him and knowing way too much about how *great* Manhattan is. But I decided to give it another go, and we hit it off in round two. In our month together, we laughed a lot, talked a great deal, and lusted after each other. But splinters showed up in our polished veneer immediately. Evan worried about anything and everything. He missed New York terribly and couldn't wait to get back "home." He was moody and feared commitment—or at least any kind of commitment to me. This got old fast. I wasn't looking for a husband, but I was looking for someone who enjoyed dating and loved jumping in the pool of experience with his best clothes on. Evan wasn't up for much more than gingerly removing his socks and toeing the water.

So he broke up with me. I saw it coming. I had hoped for a different person, and Evan set me straight. I wanted to have it out over the phone, but he insisted we talk in person. So we met up at a local bakery but skipped their famous chocolate chip cookies and got right to the topic at hand. He told me how great I was, and he seemed to mean it (or at least I decided to accept it). I expressed the hope that he'd figure out some of the things that were dogging him, and assured him I wished him only good things always. We talked about being friends in the future, and then we hugged good-bye.

It was about as different from throwing an engagement ring on a bed in an abandoned house as you can get. And in the days and weeks afterward I marveled at how good it felt to be strong enough inside that when someone called it quits I didn't simply melt. I walked away from Evan without feeling wracked. And when I realized that breaking up is just not that bad, I was instantly more open to dating for dating's sake—which is really what dating's all about. If I could enjoy myself, learn more about myself, and move on when I needed to—without fears that I'd screwed up everything and without having to lose several days to moping around in my bathrobe and best sullen expression—well, the world just got a whole lot larger.

My favorite song is a Hebrew one. It's pretty much the ancient predecessor to the Alanis Morissette song I love. It's a mere three lines, but they're sung with increasing ferocity, the third line repeated over and over as the singers bang their hands on tabletops or any available surface and stamp their feet:

The whole world is a very narrow bridge.
The important thing is
Never to be afraid.

I had been carefully making my way across that bridge, gingerly picking my steps so I wouldn't stumble and fall over the edge. But the key to getting across the bridge—as the ancient rabbis knew, Morissette knows, and after my Mr. Perfect Breakup, I learned too—is reveling in the crossing. Fear—never having the guts to cross the bridge, to date the guy, to leave the guy—is what knocks you off your feet, not the act of dating and breaking up.

Knowing how to break up is a skill you'll carry with you through life. But you'll never need it more than with Mr. Almost, the man you're sure you're going to marry—until you wise up.

Been There, Learned This

- When it's time, it's time.
- Acknowledge and respect the good stuff and forget about the rest.
- Cracking up doesn't have to follow breaking up.
- There's never a reason to *dump* someone—let him down softly and hope he returns the favor with the next woman he dates.

A THERAPIST WEIGHS IN

Ideally the breakup is not a shock but rather an evolution—here's what I'm thinking, this is my discomfort, I'm not going in this direction—so that eventually breaking up might be very sad because you have that attachment, but it's not a train wreck, it's not devastating to your self-esteem.
—Deborah Shelkrot Permut, LCSW, Psy.D.
Washington, D.C.

Check Yourself Quiz
DO YOU HAVE THE RIGHT ATTITUDE
ABOUT BREAKUPS?

Answer "Yes" or "No" to each question. Then use the scoring section to check whether Mr. Perfect Breakup is attainable for you.

_____ 1. I always eat my ice cream out of the container while crying about lost loves.

_____ 2. If I date a guy, he's forever off limits to my friends.

_____ 3. When I break up with someone, there's no going back for another round (or two) of dating.

_____ 4. I can say, "It's not you, it's me," with a straight face.

_____ 5. If I had a dollar for every guy who ever broke up with me and immediately started dating the woman he ended up marrying, I'd have a nicer car.

_____ 6. Love might make the world go round, but loving and leaving 'em keeps me on my toes.

_____ 7. I've been known to go through a box of tissues after a breakup.

_____ 8. I'm friends with some of my former boyfriends.

_____ 9. When I hear the name of an old beau in passing, my eyes well up.

_____ 10. I know just the guy, and I think he'd be amenable.

SCORING

1.	Yes: 0	No: 1	6.	Yes: 1	No: 0
2.	Yes: 0	No: 1	7.	Yes: 0	No: 1
3.	Yes: 1	No: 0	8.	Yes: 1	No: 0
4.	Yes: 1	No: 0	9.	Yes: 0	No: 1
5.	Yes: 1	No: 0	10.	Yes: 2	No: 0

0–5   Lighten up, girl!

6–7   There's hope for you. Remember: breakups are inevitable. Why not make them perfect?

8–11   You are capable of having a Mr. Perfect Breakup in your life. Enjoy! And pass the ice cream.

BREAKUP FACTS

The most interesting thing I learned in writing *There Goes the Bride* was that nearly everyone who goes through a broken engagement—whether she wanted the breakup or not, whether she was the one to call it off or not—experiences grief. Finding this out made me feel less alone and less crazy—I wanted to break up but *still* felt horrible after, and it was OK. This reaction makes sense: you're mourning the death of the future you imagined. What's typical when you're just dating and break up? David Sbarra, a University of Virginia graduate student in psychology, launched a two-year study of 300 undergrads to find out. Here are some of the facts he uncovered:

- Women are more willing to talk about their breakups. In fact Sbarra had trouble getting guys to even take part in his study. (Are you surprised?)
- Most often, breakups aren't the result of one fight or one lackluster date. People aren't that spontaneous or flip: they think their feelings through before pulling the plug. (Obviously, Sbarra didn't interview me in college.)
- People report that they start to feel better about a month after the breakup. So in the darkest hours the best advice is hang tight. Life gets better.

Bromley, A. "How Do I Love Thee? Let Me Count the Ways." *Inside UVA Online.* [www.virginia.edu/insideuva/2002/06/love.html]. Feb. 15–21, 2002.

MR. MOST PERFECT BREAKUP: BRUCE WILLIS

Demi Moore knew Bruce a mere three months before marrying him. Three kids and eleven years later they went their separate ways. Or rather they divorced; they've been spotted together so often they could hardly be called separate. The ex-husband even tags along on her dates with Ashton Kutcher. In Hollywood, where mud-slinging is as common as whirlwind breakups, theirs is truly a perfect breakup. Could you date (and leave) Bruce Willis?

PROS
- Should an asteroid hit earth or German terrorists infiltrate your office party, you're in good hands.
- He obviously cares a great deal for his kids.
- You and he can snuggle on the couch and watch those smart, funny *Moonlighting* reruns.

CONS
- Do you really want your ex along on dates with your next Mister?
- He wants to take you to Planet Hollywood for every meal.
- His ex-wife has one of the hottest bodies in Hollywood. Could you stand the comparison?

Chapter

16

Mr. Almost

I was two weeks away from marrying my Mr. Almost. Presents were piling up in the living room, and my wedding dress had been taken in and in and in. We were fourteen days away from signing on the dotted line, and very few people knew that our relationship was less than perfect. I didn't doubt wanting to date Mark, but then everything sped up and I fell beneath the wheels of the machine. I fell in love and he took care of the rest. He declared I was The One after two months of dating, and said how eager he was to start our life together. "But aren't we already together?" I asked.

He moved in after we had dated for six months. (Before dating Mark, I had never thought I would live with someone before marriage.) We were engaged after ten months (I didn't want to be engaged but then convinced myself I did. I insisted I didn't want a ring but then found myself coveting a huge rock for my finger.) We lived in a beautiful townhouse we had just bought together, but I was a shadow of myself. In the ten months we were engaged, I dropped ten pounds, suffered debilitating migraines, and tossed and turned from nightmares.

While dating Mark I lost control for the first time of what I wanted; I lost my power to speak up. With Mr. Rich and Mr. Dangerous and Mr. Smart and Mr. Not and all the other Misters, I reveled in the moment, and left when our time was over. It's not that my Mr. Almost was that persuasive or manipulative. It's that being with him made me, for the first time, question myself seriously about getting married: I was thirty, I was in love. Isn't marriage what comes next?

Ingrid thought the same way:

He was handsome and well-built, a professional ski instructor. He treated me like a princess, he made me like myself when I was with him better than I had liked myself before I met him, he pushed me to better myself for my own sake (as opposed to anybody else's), and he helped me to feel like an adult. Plus he was incredibly hot (we're being honest, right?). But I was too young, he was too old; I was too Catholic, he was too Jewish; his father hated me, my mother hated him.

So I went to Paris with my college roommate, who was engaged as well. We had both left our rings at home. We went out to dinner at a cute little cafe and proceeded to eat and drink until we thought we were going to explode. From there we went to a bar. While there we asked each other if we were going to go through with our weddings. Neither of us was willing to commit to an answer first so we wrote the answers on cocktail napkins, slid them across the table to each other, and opened them on the count of three. "One, two, three, flip!" Both napkins said, in huge, bold letters, NO! My friend started waving her wine glass wildly and calling out, "Monsieur, *s'il vous plaît*, more wine!"

FINDING THE STRENGTH

If every Mister teaches us something and leaves us with a gift, Mr. Almost taught me everything and left me with a pile of gifts on the living room floor (OK, those had to be returned, but metaphorically he did). I met Carolyn just after she had broken up with her Mr. Almost. She was depressed and furious, but she wised up pretty quickly:

Sigh. The Almost guy was tall, dark, and handsome. He seemed to have his act together with a great job. He loved my personality and wasn't intimidated by my quick wit—in fact he loved me for it. He was spontaneous and fun and made me laugh until my cheeks hurt. We were fabulously compatible in the bedroom—couldn't get enough of each other. He made me feel like the most beautiful and intelligent person on earth. At the time, I really didn't see tons of the bad about him. He was a salesman and made his living telling people what they wanted to hear, and he carried that over into his personal life. His many lies about himself and what he was doing are coming to light now, and it makes me feel like I was engaged to a stranger.

The comedy in this situation is that I realized our relationship was in trouble before we broke up, but he must have realized it at the same time and beat me to the breakup. Then I couldn't remember that he wasn't the right one anymore, and suddenly I had to have him back because he was the "only one for me"! But I wised up again .very quickly. The gradual part of it is that there are nagging thoughts in the back of your head that say, "Hey, are you really sure this is The Guy?" but you ignore them. Then one day you are driving down the road in your car and realize that you and this guy have no business getting married because you are too fundamentally different. He's not necessarily a bad person but he certainly isn't the right person.

So I went to the batting cages and hit baseballs. Went to the driving range and hit golf balls. Cried. Wrote him letters that I never sent, but I was able to pour my feelings out onto paper. Talked to friends. Found a cute rebound guy and made out with him until 5 A.M. on a trampoline. And I gained clarity about relationships—what I will and will not put up with. I learned that I am just fine alone, and I don't need someone else to make me happy.

Just as there is no Mr. Right, there is no straight path to the altar. I said yes when Mr. Almost got down on one knee and asked me to spend the next 100 years with him because he was lovely, he was fun, and I thought he was someone I could travel the world with. Now, all those reasons are as weighty as sand through my fingers.

When you are presented with a choice between a Mr. Almost and an immediate future all by yourself, it takes an inordinate amount of strength to choose the latter. It takes more strength than I thought I had in those days to say: "I love him, but not forever." That's not the way our parents think of love and not the way fairy tales work. If you love him, society says you marry him. But it's not always that simple:

He was a "relaxed agnostic," in his own words. He was cute and we were both interested in sci-fi books. He was different than most guys. Besides, I felt motherly toward him. He made me challenge every belief and thought I ever had. I think that his manipulation of me into following his thoughts and beliefs was a way to justify his way of thinking. I feel like he was a lost soul that needed guidance. I thought I could give him guidance, but instead I lost myself. I agreed to marry him two weeks after meeting him. It was crazy, but I loved—at the time—how he challenged me. My parents and friends hated him. I never doubted that he loved me and still does some-where. It just isn't the love that would have made a marriage work.

—*Melinda*

CONTINUING TO GROW

My Mr. Almost, frightened by my ambivalence, called off our wedding. It's not too simplistic to say a weight was lifted from me. I went through grief and wrote *There Goes the Bride* as my catharsis, but at the end of the journey I finally fully believed in myself, and I expanded to my full capacity. Mr. Almost is the final Mister in the mix because, I realized, getting married isn't—can't be—the purpose in my life. Now it's not just that I got over my painful breakups (and whether you get over your pain is up to you), it's that I'm actually glad for them. I'm glad for the experiences that resulted in the pain, and I'm glad for the pain, because you don't move for-ward on the fine days. Life sometimes jolts the hell out of you, but when you master the bump, you've moved further than you ever thought you could.

Mr. Almost isn't a Mister I would necessarily recommend seeking out like the others. But he's one many of us will end up sampling nonetheless. If you date a Mr. Almost, remember to listen to your instincts, don't forget what you need, and have patience with yourself as you recover from him.

Now that I think about it, you can't go wrong with any Mister if you keep those rules in mind. I want you to ride the roller-coaster—just remember to fasten your seat belt. It's a helluva ride.

Been There, Learned This

- When my body is falling apart, it's actually jumping up and down, waving banners, trying to get my mind to listen.
- Life isn't a game of musical chairs. It's not as if the music stops at age thirty and I have to marry the guy I'm dating right then.
- Mr. Almost, like all the other Misters, is meant to be enjoyed and then moved on from.

A THERAPIST WEIGHS IN

In my practice I see women who notice the little things building up and then it's an "Aha!" moment—she realizes he's not The One.
—Ruth Greer, Ph.D.
Rye, New York

Check Yourself Quiz
IS HE A MR. ALMOST?

Answer "Yes" or "No" to each question. Then use the scoring section to check whether your Mister is a Mr. Almost.

_____ 1. If he changed just one thing about himself, he'd be perfect.

_____ 2. We argue regularly about one or two issues.

_____ 3. When I close my eyes I can see the rest of my life with this guy.

_____ 4. I find myself telling friends, "I love him, but . . ."

_____ 5. He wants to get married. I want to stay like this.

_____ 6. I've been dreaming about an old boyfriend.

_____ 7. He's a momma's boy.

_____ 8. He's in love with the idea of love.

_____ 9. He prefers me in full makeup.

_____ 10. I'm not sure if it's cold feet or something more, but I feel all wrong and I'm scared.

SCORING

1.	Yes: 1	No: 0	6.	Yes: 1	No: 0
2.	Yes: 1	No: 0	7.	Yes: 1	No: 0
3.	Yes: 0	No: 1	8.	Yes: 1	No: 0
4.	Yes: 1	No: 0	9.	Yes: 1	No: 0
5.	Yes: 1	No: 0	10.	Yes: 2	No: 0

0–5 He's probably not Mr. Almost. Sounds more like you could have the makings of a life partner here.

6–7 This relationship could go either way. Take your time deciding.

8–11 Lace on your running sneakers.

THE AMAZING OPPORTUNITY

Nobody gives better advice on appreciating and getting over Mr. Almost then those of us who almost married him. Here's some hard-won wisdom from some Almost Brides—women who have been through a broken engagement:

> Even though it feels like your life has been ruined, you've actually just been given an amazing opportunity—the opportunity to find your own identity again. You are going to come out on the other side of this a stronger, smarter, and much happier person.
> —*Sophie*

> If this was not the right relationship for you, you have just done the most courageous thing you could have done.
> —*Elly*

> No amount of effort is going to make a relationship work if it's not meant to be. In my case it wasn't meant to be at all, but I didn't want to see it, so I tried and tried. Then when it didn't work, I blamed myself. Do not take all the responsibility on yourself. When something ends, it's because it wasn't meant to be. You can't blame yourself for that. You don't have that kind of power. Most importantly, don't give up on love.
> —*Samantha*

Excerpted from Safier, R., with Roberts, W. *There Goes the Bride.* San Francisco: Jossey-Bass, 2003.

MR. ALMOST: TATE DONOVAN

Jennifer Aniston's alter-ego Rachel Green knows about Mr. Almost. This *Friends* character bolted on her wedding day, leaving her rich-but-boring fiancé at the altar. And Aniston's real-life fiancé, Tate Donovan, was the recipient of her experience. According to various fan Web sites, Donovan felt overshadowed by Aniston's rising star (he couldn't take previous girlfriend's Sandra Bullock's success either). Aniston eventually had enough. Some reports say that when push came to shove, she told the self-esteem-threatened Donovan that if he didn't come to her *Object of My Affection* premiere, they were over. He didn't show up. Want a slightly used Mr. Almost?

PROS
- Loves biking and B&Bs (he has groused that the high-maintenance Ms. Aniston preferred luxury accommodations).
- With his sweet smile and curly mop-top, Donovan was named one of the ten sexiest Broadway stars of 1999.
- His exes go on to great fame and fortune. It's as if he's a magnet for the up-and-coming.

CONS
- God forbid you have an ambitious bone in your body. And if you get famous he'll pout.
- He hasn't been named sexiest anything since '99.
- Tate who?

Epilogue

I went out to the suburbs the other night to see two of my favorite people and their two kids and their dog. I love going there, not just because I love my friends but because it's such a haven. I hug and kiss kids and dog and listen to the two-year-old sing "Itsy-Bitsy Spider" and we all run in circles and flop around on the grass and gravely watch the dog poop and read books about kindly dinosaurs and gorillas who want to sleep in bed with the zookeeper and not in their boring cages. In my day-to-day life I don't do a single one of these things.

Last night the baby refused to go down for the night, so while Daria cooed to her, Stuart and I hung out in the kitchen, sucking on all-natural apple juice Popsicles, catching up. Then Daria drove me to the Metro so *we* would have a chance to talk (dinner was all about singing), and we ended up sitting in the car at the station and talking about my recently deceased dad, whom I miss so much I ache, and what life brings and will bring.

It's funny the way our lives work out. There was a time when Daria was single too, and (though I'm not sure she can remember it now) she slept late and ate cereal for dinner and could throw herself into work without worrying about what time day care closed. Her life then was all about her, as she readily admits. She dated Mr. Right Nows, and she had a wonderful time. Then she met Stuart in the copy room of their office, and as Stuart tells it, it was as if they had always known each other. Now, five years married, they have their fantastic kids, and, Daria says, the kids, just naturally, come first. She says it with neither regret nor enthusiasm—it's obvious how deep her love is for her children, but as she told another couple who were talking about starting a family, you really have to be ready for it. She was ready. And her life, her minivan, and her nights and weekends of singing and bath time and kisses and exhaustion are exactly what she wants.

And then Daria turned to me and said: "I am always right about these things. And I see you married, and if not with a kid then expecting one, in less than five years."

I guess statistically that makes sense. But she could have said, "Now, get yourself to California, without a car, bus, train, or airplane," for as much as I could comprehend it. It's as if her life is parallel to mine and there are no roads that cross over.

Since I wrote *There Goes The Bride,* I've been wondering about these different kinds of lives. Pretty much daily I check in with myself: What do I want? What do I need? I've spoken to hundreds of women with broken engagements, and initially, nearly every single one is terrified that she'll never find a man to marry, that maybe we all get one shot and her one shot fell in love with his secretary or bored her to tears and, *ping!* time's up. Thanks for playing. Please step to the back of the line. Women ask what I'm working on now, and when I tell them about *Mr. Right Now* they all say, "Oh! I need that!" As if without a good shake we can't recall what's so great about our own rich lives.

I forget sometimes too. I'll stay out late, sleep in, work all day, go for a run and then, out in the suburbs, think: I want to own a home. I want to be in love forever.

But it's not a straight shot from here to there. If it were, our divorce rate wouldn't be so high. If it were, you would relax into your life now and trust that you'll have another life sometime later.

I know women who sincerely feel that because they aren't married yet, their lives suck. One book can't make society stop heralding marriage as if it's the wonder cure for loneliness and self-doubt. One ranting writer on a soapbox can't make all your fears disappear. My hope is that this one book from the hands of this ranting writer can make you stop beating yourself up and wishing yourself exhausted. You aren't running in place. You haven't lost in the game of life. You're getting there—wherever "there" is for you.

I decided to set my thoughts and experiences to paper after Jossey-Bass published *There Goes the Bride* last spring. Immediately, women began to send me worried, desperate letters. What if they let this guy go? How could they know there'd be another guy behind him? This book is my response. There *are* other guys ("There's another streetcar coming along in ten minutes," as my grandmother used to put it to my mother), and I've described some of my favorites.

Marriage will come in time, if you choose it. No reason to rush, and many reasons—and Misters—to insist on *not* rushing. I hope this book has gone a ways toward lessening your stress. It has certainly been fun to research. Enjoy yours!

Best,
Rachel Safier

Notes

INTRODUCTION

1. *Publishers Weekly,* Aug. 25, 2003.

2. Walsh, W. L. *The Boyfriend Test: How to Evaluate His Potential Before You Lose Your Heart.* New York: Three Rivers Press, 2001, p. 247.

3. Whitehead, B. D. *Why There Are No Good Men Left: The Romantic Plight of the New Single Woman.* New York: Broadway Books, 2003, p. 14.

4. Ehrenreich, B. "Why It Might Be Worth It (to Have an Affair)." In D. Chasman and C. Jhee (eds.), *Here Lies My Heart: Essays on Why We Marry, Why We Don't, and What We Find There.* Boston: Beacon Press, 1999, p. 60.

5. Paul, P. *The Starter Marriage and the Future of Matrimony.* New York: Villard Books, 2002, p. 105.

6. Roiphe, K. *Last Night in Paradise: Sex and Morals at the Century's End.* Boston: Little, Brown, 1997, pp. 28–29.

7. Blackwell, A. B. "Divorce Laws Should Not Be Liberalized." In B. Stalcup (ed.), *The Women's Rights Movement: Opposing Viewpoints.* San Diego, Calif.: Greenhaven Press, 1996, p. 106.

CHAPTER ONE

1. Faludi, S. *Backlash: The Undeclared War Against American Women.* New York: Anchor Books, 1992, p. 14.

2. U.S. Census Bureau. "Women Closing the Gap with Men in Some Measures, According to Census Bureau." [www.

census.gov/Press-Release/www/2003/cb03–53.html], Mar. 24, 2003.

3. Whitehead, B. D. *Why There Are No Good Men Left: The Romantic Plight of the New Single Woman.* New York: Broadway Books, 2003, pp. 7, 59.

4. Whitehead, 2003, p. 39.

5. Faludi, 1992, p. 14.

6. Paul, P. *The Starter Marriage and the Future of Matrimony.* New York: Villard Books, 2002, p. 39.

7. Faludi, 1992, p. 37.

8. Paul, 2002, p. 239.

9. Kipnis, L. *Against Love: A Polemic.* New York: Pantheon Books, 2003.

10. Brady, L. *Love Lessons: Twelve Real-Life Love Stories.* New York: Simon & Schuster, 1999, p. 169.

11. Wallerstein, J. S., and Blakeslee, S. *The Good Marriage: How and Why Love Lasts.* Boston: Houghton Mifflin, 1995, p. 101.

12. Friedan, B. *The Feminine Mystique.* New York: Norton, 1983, p. 291. (Originally published 1963)

13. Orenstein, P. *Flux: Women on Sex, Work, Kids, Love and Life in a Half-Changed World.* New York: Doubleday, 2000, p. 241.

14. Friedan, 1983, p. 67.

15. Beauvoir, S. de. *The Second Sex.* New York: Vintage Books, 1989, p. 137. (Originally published 1952)

16. Whitehead, 2003, p. 42.

17. Whitehead, 2003, p. 58.

18. Quoted in Ehrenreich, B. "The Women's Movement, Feminists and AntiFeminists." *Radical America,* Spring 1981, *15*(1–2), p. 98; Rowbotham, S. *A Century of Women: The History of Women in Britain and the United States.* New York: Viking Penguin, 1997, p. 443.

19. Whitehead, 2003, p. 105.

20. Whitehead, 2003, p. 153.

21. "She Kept the Dress," *Toronto National Post,* Mar. 5, 2003.

22. Schwartz, P. *Everything You Know About Love and Sex Is Wrong: Twenty-Five Relationship Myths Redefined to Achieve Happiness and Fulfillment in Your Intimate Life.* New York: Putnam, 2000, p. 52.

23. Miles, R. *The Women's History of the World.* Topsfield, Mass.: Salem House, 1989, p. 116.

24. Yalom, M. *A History of the Wife.* New York: HarperCollins, 2001, p. xii.

CHAPTER TWO

1. Anna Rosner, personal communication to the author, Aug. 2003.

2. Larson, J. *Should We Stay Together: A Scientifically Proven Method for Evaluating Your Relationship and Improving Its Chances for Long-Term Success.* Jossey-Bass, 2000, p. 4.

3. Larson, 2000, p. 4.

CHAPTER SIX

1. Heyn, D. *Marriage Shock: The Transformation of Women into Wives.* New York: Villard, 1997, p 157.

CHAPTER EIGHT

1. Houston, J. *The Possible Human: A Course in Extending Your Physical, Mental, and Creative Abilities.* Los Angeles: Tarcher, 1997.

CHAPTER NINE

1. Golden, F. "Person of the Century." *Time*, Jan. 3, 2000. © 2000 TIME Inc. Reprinted by permission.

CHAPTER ELEVEN

1. Kantrowitz, B. "Hoping for the Best, Ready for the Worst." *Newsweek*, May 12, 2003.

2. "Forbes World's Richest People: 2002." [www.forbes.com/billionaires2002/home.html?passListId=10&passYear=2002&passListType=Person], 2002.

CHAPTER TWELVE

1. See [www.dictionary.com].

2. Healy, J. R. "Nissan Pours on the Macho." *USA Today*, July 24, 2000.

3. Lawton, W. "Hey, Fellas: Operation Tries to Get Guys into Nursing." *Oregonian*, Nov. 14, 2002.

CHAPTER THIRTEEN

1. Anna Rosner, personal communication to the author, Aug. 2003.

2. Rosner, Aug. 2003.

3. Williamson, M. *A Woman's Worth*. New York: Ballantine, 1994, p. 59.

CHAPTER FOURTEEN

1. Shalit, W. *A Return to Modesty: Discovering the Lost Virtue*. New York: Free Press, 1999, p. 138.

2. Miles, R. *The Women's History of the World.* Topsfield, Mass.: Salem House, 1989, p. 105.

3. Quoted in Paul, P. *The Starter Marriage and the Future of Matrimony.* New York: Villard Books, 2002, p. 238.

4. Stossel, S. "The Sexual Counterrevolution." *The American Prospect,* July 1–Aug. 1, 1997, *8*(33).

5. "Playboy Interview: Colin Farrell." *Playboy,* Mar. 2003.

About the Author

Rachel Safier is a journalist who has written for magazines, television, and the Web. She is the author of *There Goes the Bride: Making Up Your Mind, Calling It Off, and Moving On* and the founder of the Web site theregoesthebride.com.